A BISHOP in SNEAKERS

Also by Owen E Clark MD
through Amazon Direct Publishing

Nursery Stories: Lessons for Life

Copyright © 2018 by Owen E Clark MD

All rights reserved, including the right to reproduce this book or portions thereof in any form whatsoever. If you would like permission to use material from this book (other than for review purposes), please contact the author at 310 Morton Street, Ashland, OR 97520.

ISBN: 9781717788054 (paperback)

First print edition: December 2018
First ebook edition: December 2018

Printed in the United States of America

A BISHOP in SNEAKERS

Sermons from the Mormon pulpit

Owen E Clark MD

The followings talks are from a collection of sermons given by one bishop in one place and time. It reflects a combination of the generic approach many bishops take and also the unique background Bishop Clark brings to this calling.

For 8½ years Owen E. Clark adjusted his schedule for rounding on a psychiatric inpatient unit to accommodate his Sunday church schedule. His words draw upon his own upbringing in a southeast Idaho Mormon settlement, his advanced schooling on both coasts (Harvard, U Washington, U Oregon, Yale) and his practice as a psychiatrist.

These talks from the pulpit are shaped by the needs of the congregation: members ranging from older, often widowed, inner-city saints to graduate students at the university struggling to reconcile their traditional beliefs with their academic challenges. They draw upon Bishop Clark's interest in history and science (his college studies), his dedication to his wife, Barbara (mother of three children and a pediatric oncologist), and his striving to understand the needs, hopes and fears of his patients.

All of the following sermons were given to Bishop Clark's congregation in north Seattle, with the exception of one talk at a near-by congregation, notes from a training session promoted by the stake president for the bishops under his ecclesiastic hand, and a "written report" on the nursery following his release as bishop after serving 8½ years.

CONTENTS

Preface: A Bishop in Sneakers
Explanatory note on the nature of a Mormon Bishop

In the Beginning   1
1 – Appreciation and comments
2 – Rights of the priesthood
3 – Pray by name

The Church of Saints
The Society of Saints   5
4 – On gossiping and backbiting
5 – Missing members
6 – Notes on counseling by bishops
7 – The Church

Building Zion   16
8 – Reflections on leadership
9 – Pattern your life
10 – To bring our brethren again to Thee
11 – What we make of it

Living the Gospel   31
12 – Meaning of temple work
13 – Follow the prophet
14 – Laws and commandments of the gospel
15 – The duties of members
16 – Two kinds of cookies; two sets of books

Personal Worship
Walk With God   51
17 – In the year that Uzziah died
18 – Your personal relationship with God
19 – The foundation of our life

Our Divinity   60
20 – Wrought upon and cleansed
21 – Understanding our relationship to scripture

Eternal Striving   66
22 – On sacrifice
23 – The sound of *shin*
24 – The short cut; do you really think there is one?
25 – A question without an answer
26 – Let us labor diligently
27 – Quiet and assurance forever

The Annual Cycle
Christmas   89
28 – Jesus comes
29 – Mary's burden
30 – Shepherds in the field
31 – A babe in swaddling clothes
32 – Jesus of Nazareth

Easter   109
33 – The day before Easter
34 – The message of Easter
35 – The fullness of the resurrection

Mother's Day — 118
36 – The mother's sacrifice

Funeral Addresses — 123
37 – God's grace in a time of loss
38 – The binding of generations
39 – The fullness of life
40 – Preaching to the choir

At the End — 136
41 – Upon being released
42 – Report: The nursery routine
43 – Afterthought: On church governance

Listing of sermons by date given — 147

Preface

A Bishop in Sneakers
Published in Sunstone, vol. 135 (Dec., 2004), pp. 10-11
by Sarah Ray Allred, Seattle, Washington
Reprinted here by permission of the author.

About five years ago, I moved from Provo to Seattle, Washington, for graduate school. My church experiences in Provo had been difficult. I'm a member of the "Borderlands," to use the term D. Jeff Burton coined for his SUNSTONE column, and I'd felt a bit isolated in Provo. I eagerly hoped to move into a ward where I could feel a sense of spiritual and social community.

The first hint that my new ward would be different from my Provo ward was when the bishop's son came to help us move in and mentioned that he was planning to study theology in graduate school. This impression was strengthened on my first Sunday when I noticed that every member of the bishopric had facial hair! I later learned that it was a running joke in the ward: any man who wanted a leadership position should grow a beard.

A few weeks later, during an emotionally difficult time, I left sacrament meeting a few minutes early in tears. A sister had chosen to speak about priesthood and had given an exceptionally authoritarian talk. She insisted that obedience to the priesthood included dutifully submitting to all requests by all priesthood holders, even when that request was as mundane as a husband's food preferences. In Utah, I just shrugged such talks off, but I had come with hope that things might be different here. That night, the bishop called, asking to meet with me. With trepidation, I drove to his home that evening, wondering if his call that night were merely a coincidence. When I walked into his study, he asked how I was doing and said he noticed I had left sacrament meeting early. He paused for a few moments. I said nothing, either. Then he spoke, softly, contemplatively. He said that he had considered stepping up to the stand after this sister's talk to disagree with her, but he felt that people should be allowed to speak their minds, even if not everyone agreed. At first, I couldn't believe my ears. The bishop didn't hold that men alone had all the authority? The bishop thought that we should be allowed to express dissent? Either one was a bombshell, but together the statements were nothing short of miraculous!

A few months later, I was invited to join a small discussion group that met once a month at the bishop's home. The subject, not too unusual, was a New Testament commentary. The unusual part is that this particular commentary had been written by Friedrich Weinreb, a Ph.D. economist imbued in the ancient Jewish tradition, and that the reading was my bishop's own translation from the original German. I looked forward to that monthly meeting, where we discussed points from the commentary and how it related to the Mormon perspective.

This bishop admitted that he and other leaders were not always inspired and could make mistakes. He has published articles in Dialogue, and I've heard him disagree, privately, with men above him in the Church's hierarchy. He reminded me that I was not the only one in the Church or even in our ward who sometimes found certain doctrinal and cultural issues troublesome. For the first time in my life, I felt I had a bishop in whom I could confide without carefully measuring my words.

Sometimes I find it frustrating that I clutch small signs of nonconformity with such fervor. Honestly, what does it really matter if I've seen the bishop come to church wearing white sneakers colorfully emblazoned with the names of all the Primary children, or if he joked one Sunday that he expected me to be with a six-pack down at the lake watching boat races instead of sitting decorously in Relief Society? For whatever reason, this bishop's individuality and humor set up an environment that encouraged spiritual growth for me, and, I believe, for most of the ward.

The time of my move to Seattle coincided with a personal crisis of faith. Because of my frustrations with institutional practices, I had allowed my personal relationship with God to languish. I will forever be grateful to this bishop whose kind and wise leadership allowed me time and space to foster my testimony of core gospel principles. I now feel my beliefs are strong enough that I can actively create a nurturing spiritual environment instead of being entirely shaped by my surroundings. Without the church experience shaped in large part by this bishop, I'm not sure if I would have found that strength.

This man is no longer the bishop, and I'm not sure I'll ever have another ecclesiastical leader quite like him. But I'm comforted to know that he's continuing to shape the church's future — his last act as bishop was to arrange to have himself called as a worker in the Primary nursery, where he has remained for the past two years.

Explanatory note on the nature of a Mormon Bishop

A bishop in the Church of Jesus Christ of Latter-day Saints holds a unique position. It is roughly equivalent to a Catholic parish priest. Unlike the trained and paid ministry of other religions, a Mormon bishop contributes his service for a limited period of time, commonly five or so years, and receives neither professional training nor financial compensation. He is expected to support himself and his family, usually through his regular occupation, while functioning as the leading officer of his congregation.

Mormons hold that their bishop, and all other church leaders, are called of God. Operationally, his name is proposed by the leaders in the local church hierarchy, vetted by the general church authorities, and presented to the local congregation to be "sustained" by the members of the congregation, their approval given by their upraised hands — which is usually a pro forma practice.

The bishop is the presiding head of the local congregation, which is called a "ward." In Mormonism, this is a group usually composed of some 200 or so "active" families, whose membership is determined by their residence — with exceptions made only by permission of ecclesiastical authorities. This means that all Mormons residing in a given area are expected to attend and participate in the local congregation. So practically, if a person is discontent with his bishop he may either withdraw from active church participation, move his residence to another ward, or wait until a new bishop is chosen. This gives the ward the quality of a family with its innate membership, rather than a voluntary association as in most other American social organizations.

Upon being called, a bishop usually is given a brief orientation by the former bishop, receives advice from his immediate superior in the church hierarchy, the stake president (akin to a bishop in a Catholic diocese), and is handed the church handbook for bishops, which outlines guiding principles on the administration of the ward. He may also receive counsel from the leadership of the stake and training sessions from higher-ups in the church organization. Finally, he is subject to an abundance of free advice from anyone who has the temerity to tell the bishop how to fulfill his calling.

In the Mormon church most all active members participate in the operation of the church organization. They do so by assignment, i.e., by calling, of the bishopric. The bishop has two counselors whom he chooses from his congregation, subject to approval of higher church authority and the sustaining vote of the congregation — both of which are usually given pro forma. The bishopric assigns ("calls") the leaders and teachers of his ward, e.g. the Relief Society presidency for the women, the Primary presidency for the children, the organist and chorister, etc. In Mormon culture most participating ("active") healthy-bodied members are expected to accept some "calling," i.e., position in the church, and to serve until released by the authority that called them, again for a limited period of time and without financial compensation.

At the time of Bishop Clark's service the core of contemporary Mormon church service was a three-hour block on Sunday which features three consecutive meetings. The Sacrament Meeting is characterized by church members partaking of the sacrament of the Lord's supper, the singing of hymns, and 30 to 40 minutes of talks from the pulpit, usually sermons by either local church authorities or lay members of the congregation, who speak on invitation of the bishopric, either on an assigned topic or one of their own choosing. Members then meet in a Sunday School which include classes for adolescents and Primary classes for children. Finally, the male adults and adolescents meet in a Priesthood meeting which includes a lesson, while the women have corresponding Relief Society and Young Women meetings.

The bishop has oversight responsibility for the entire ward. This involves a particular assignment to administer church funds received and distributed in the ward. These includes "fast offerings" (the monetary equivalent of two meals which faithful members forgo once a month) specified for the poor in the ward. He is specifically charged to provide leadership and guidance to the youth. He is their primary spiritual counselor, and, by some members, is looked to as a marital counselor, family therapist and business and financial advisor

He is a "judge in Israel," who is charged to maintain church order and discipline. He has the discretion to call a "Bishop's Court", and (with his counselors) pass ecclesiastic judgment, e.g. in cases of sexual transgressions and grossly unseemly behavior. He and his counselors interview all members (yearly at that period of time) who wish to attend the Mormon temple and to participate in temple ordinances.

If that were not enough, he is to give sermons from the pulpit on a regular basis. In practice, a bishop has great discretion in how often he speaks and on what topics. Given that he, assisted by his counselors, assigns all church talks, he could give a sermon whenever. In practice, many bishops confine their remarks to every third month when presiding at the ward fast and testimony meeting, and at the annual ward conference when the stake leadership makes its formal annual visit. Finally, the bishop usually arranges funeral services of ward members and is frequently asked by the family to speak.

Every bishop has his unique life history, his own style, his own predilections, likes and dislikes. He has wide-ranging discretion in giving voice to them, and is effectively limited only by direct intervention by higher church authority or the social pressure of his peers and ward members.

A note on references to scripture. In addition to the books of the Old and New Testament the Church of Jesus Christ of Latter-day Saints recognizes as scripture the Doctrine and Covenants (D&C), and books in the Book of Mormon, e.g., Nephi, Mosiah, Alma, and Moroni.

In the Beginning

In the first weeks after a new Mormon bishop is called and sustained, curious members try to "read the tea leaves" from early pronouncements from the pulpit and any changes in the organization of leadership.

1 Appreciation and comments
Upon being sustained - 8/08/93

Changes come in the church, and now it's come to this. The first thing to change is that I quit making smart-aleck remarks about "the first thing I'll do when I'm bishop."

Seriously, I must voice my appreciation:

to my wife for many things, which I'll express in private;

to my three children whose curiosity, daring, intensity, and persistence has expanded my horizons, warmed my heart, and made my hair turn gray;

to my elders (of both sexes) of several generations who have given me an upright example, protection and encouragement;

to my fellow-saints (including those sitting here in this room), none of whom I'll embarrass by mentioning by name.

to past and present bishops and stake presidents who have recognized my need through the years up to now for time to pursue other things I've needed to do.

to Bishop Allred for all that he has done, for his not leaving many loose ends to tidy up, for having more love and caring than might have always been appreciated by everyone in the ward.

You've noticed, I trust, that this bishopric is relatively inexperienced. We have a steep learning curve ahead; we have a lot to learn in a hurry. In this we ask for your patience and your prayers. I figure this deficit will be overcome by so many able ward workers, whom I will ask to continue in their present callings for now, and by the good will and good works which abound in this ward.

2 Rights of the Priesthood
Priesthood Correlation Meeting - 8/22/93

"...the rights of the priesthood are inseparably connected with the powers of heaven..." (D&C 121:36)

All that we do in any official capacity here in this room, in this building, in this Church is by right of the priesthood. That right does not exist other than in its connection with the powers of heaven. Our activities in the Church of Jesus Christ have no legitimacy and no efficacy other than in that connection. If we lose that connection to the powers of heaven at any time, in any act, in any utterance, in any thought, in any feeling, we lose the rights of the priesthood and we act, talk, think and feel on our own, and will show ourselves to the ward and the world as the charming, lovable, foolish children that we are.

We have been called to the offices in which we here serve, but we will not be included among the chosen unless we learn this one lesson: we can act in the priesthood only in accord with the powers of heaven. I pray that the questions I put and the responses I give are always in accord with these powers. I would have no goal other than this. (Incidentally, goal is not a scriptural word; it is not found in any of the standard works – except in the plural form in the TOPICAL GUIDE with reference to Objectives, which likewise is not found in the text of any scripture.) The powers of heaven need us — as we need them. We are interconnected. I do believe we are to serve as the hands and mouth of God in this portion of the vineyard. May this connection sustain us, may our belief in the connection steady us, and may our faith in this connection enrich us. This I pray.

3 Pray by name
Comments in Sacrament Meeting - 8/22/93

I would testify, that is, I would speak from my own experience, of two things. One is the mantle of ordination. The second is the efficacy and power of prayer, particularly of prayer by name.

If it seems strange to you to call me "bishop", think how much more so it is for me. I acknowledge it as a sign of respect, and am mindful that it is respect for the office of the bishop, not for me individually. I am no more, nor less, worthy of respect than I was two weeks ago. I am aware that in the last two weeks I have taken on a different personae. I am the same person, but the personage that relates to you in the office of bishop is different. I wouldn't try to define this any further, but I tell you I know something is different.

In ordaining and setting me apart as bishop, President Tucker voiced that people were praying for me by name. I feel that, and I am grateful for that. I thank you for your prayers; our ward is better for this.

I have one request of you in this regard. If and when you are moved to pray for me by name, I ask that you include at least one other person in your prayer. Pray for Sue Higbee who as president of the Relief Society carries the responsibility for leadership and coordination of work with the sisters of the ward. Pray for John Biehl by name, who as group leader of the High Priests carries the responsibility for all the older members of the ward. Pray for Chris Erickson by name, who as Elders' Quorum president carries a similar responsibility for the younger members of the ward. Pray for your visiting teachers by name. Pray for your home teachers by name. And if you do not know the names of your visiting teachers or home teachers, call up one of the above persons and inquire who they are.

The prayers of an honest heart do make a difference. And prayer by name makes a particular difference.

The Church of Saints

The Society of Saints

Mormons have more organic cohesion than most American religious congregations because of a host of factors: a history of persecution; a wariness on the part of other religious groups because of Mormon's unique beliefs and practices and Mormon's vigorous proselyting efforts; social pressure within the church to conform in practice and belief. Being more tightly-knit, relationships and feelings, both positive and negative, are more intense.

4 On gossiping and backbiting
Sacrament Meeting – 9/12/93

For the last several days I've been reading and re-reading the qualifications to serve as bishop. The most apt texts I've found are 1 Timothy 3:2 and Titus 1:7. Both have a list, and both lists begin with a declaration that a bishop must be blameless. I am still stuck there.

I am not blameless. I never have been blameless. I don't suppose that I ever will be blameless. But I do believe in repentance and forgiveness. Here's the deal: I'll work at repentance if you will exercise forgiveness.

Toward this end I have one specific request. If anyone here has been offended by me, please take it up with me. Do so personally, and do so sooner than not. I am mindful when we humans live together, we can easily rub one another the wrong way. Indeed, I think it is inevitable. If I haven't offended you, I surely will — sooner or later. Please take your offense up with me, personally, and please do so sooner rather than later. Call the executive secretary and schedule an appointment to call me to repentance.

And whenever someone else starts to tell you of my short-comings, protect yourself from being party to malicious gossip by doing two things. First, say: "Don't tell me; tell Bishop Clark; he needs to know this so he can mend his ways." And also tell the other person: "I'm impressed by your giving serious thought to the needs of the ward. Know that I am going to call the ward executive secretary and leave a message that you will be calling to set up an appointment with Bishop Clark and it should be given a high priority."

I ask you to do this not just for my sake but to protect you from the sin of being party to gossip. I ask this so we may not allow discord within the ward that keeps us from being one. "If ye are not one, ye are not mine," and if we are not His, we are nothing, our work is of no eternal worth.

5 Missing members
Sacrament Meeting – 12/19/93

Attending the funeral of Rudy Allred this last week has been the Lord's way of giving me cause to reflect upon "missing members." I've missed Rudy since he moved out of our ward. I miss his questions in priesthood meeting. They were honest, real and probing; they weren't settled by some standard pat answer.

I carry the image of his wife, now facing life as a single person for the first time since age 16. I can only begin to imagine what it must be like to see the casket carrying your loved one being wheeled out of the door of church towards the hearse headed to the cemetery.

We first become aware of what we have when it is missing. I was reminded of this the last time I bruised a finger. For the following three days it seemed as if I used that particular digit in almost all my manual operations.

This also applies to the limbs and digits of the body of Christ of which we are a part. As long as Joseph Vance was here every Sunday, appointments with the bishop just got made. Only when he's gone for a couple of weeks does the enquiry arise, "How do I make an appointment?" (Incidentally, in regard to this matter, Winston Burke, the ward clerk, is here this week, last week, and every week — and he is available for scheduling).

These matters remind me that it is people that we miss. We become aware of how much people mean to us when they are no longer in our immediate presence. The same does not apply to numbers representing aggregates of populations. Truth be told, I do not miss the 62% of our ward membership who essentially have never been seen inside of this building. Not that members on church rolls who do not meet with us do not count, but they are not part of my emotional life. They do count when I take occasion to visit them in their homes, or when I know them from some other context. I'm not saying that the people don't count; I'm just saying that I lack the emotional attachment to "statistics" that I have to people with whom I have had personal contact. For me, this brings up an existential question: can we miss what we have never experienced?

One of joys of sitting on the stand is to see faces come through the back doors into the chapel. (This joy tends to offset the ecclesiastical duty to appear to stay awake while sitting on the stand.) Parallel to this joy is the other feeling which arises in me when one of those faces does not appear at the chapel door.

I am not moved by nameless "statistics," but I am moved by those saints whom I home teach, with whom I have had recent contact, who are on my mind and my heart.

And herein I need your help, and your fellow saints need your help. Four hundred people is not a large congregation for a full-time cleric, nor inordinately large for a young man with an outgoing nature, good memory and boundless energy. But... you see the problem. Now, if everyone sitting here were to take personal responsibility for, say, a half-dozen families, get to know them, be mindful when they're sick or out of town, or discouraged or disgusted — then no one need get lost in the crowd.

I am mindful that as home teachers or visiting teachers we may lapse momentarily in remembrance of our charges. But repentance is always in order. And we have the reassurance that there is never a lapse in awareness by our loving Father above.

In this matter we may find assurance in the Word. In the Book of Moses (Pearl of Great Price: Moses 7:29-33) we find a remarkable query by Enoch:

"And Enoch said unto the Lord: How is it that thou canst weep, seeing thou art holy, and from all eternity to all eternity?

"... and naught but peace, justice, and truth is the habitation of thy throne; ... how is it thou canst weep?

And the Lord tells him the cause of His divine tears.

"The Lord said unto Enoch: Behold these thy brethren; they are the workmanship of mine own hands...

"And unto thy brethren have I said, and also given commandment, that they should love one another, and that they should choose me, their Father. ..."

God weeps for us, for we are the work of His own hands. When we weep for our fellow mankind, we join God in acknowledging that we are all children of a loving God. And in our tears, we follow the way of our loving God. Might it even be said that we herewith act in God's stead. Might this in part be what is described in the Doctrine and Covenants 84:100:

"...The Lord hath gathered all things in one.

The Lord hath brought down Zion from above.

The Lord hath brought up Zion from beneath."

Just as the Lord gathers us, may we join in gathering our fellow saints, those who are missing the joy we together share.

6 Notes on counseling by Bishops
Seattle North Stake
Presidency/Bishopric Meeting — 1/06/94

BE YOURSELF
Speak from your own position and life experience.
Who you are determines your own particular style and approach.

Allow the working of the Spirit through you.
The Lord knows whom He has called; He will work with you.
Be alert to prompting and "passing thoughts."

Don't presume authority or inspiration more than you have.
Don't invoke your office or the name of the Lord unless clearly moved to do so.

USE ACTIVE RESTRAINT
Hear a person out until what you are told makes its own kind of sense.
Hold back judgment until you can see how a person could act like they did.
Don't jump in with premature imputation of motive.

Remember that being heard out often helps more than being told something.
"I hear you" often counts more than "Here's the answer."

Give people time to work out their own solutions to their problems.

You may ask: "What do you think ought to be done here?"

You may say: "Let's think about this; come back next week with your best options."

KEEP BOUNDARIES

Be clear what is for the good of the one you counsel, and what is to make yourself feel comfortable or the Church look good.

Don't be seduced.

Not by adoration, praise, or threats (e.g., self-harm or blackmail).

Be circumspect.

Never give occasion for accusations of improper conduct.

Counsel girls, women (and vulnerable males) only when someone is in the next room.

ASK FOR HELP

Use other church resources fully (while respecting confidentiality).

Consider involvement of home and visiting teachers and quorum leaders.

Consider existing church programs: Single Adults, Deseret Industries, L.D.S. Social Services.

Use community resources.

Governmental and volunteer service agencies exist to provide services.

Get personal support and help, particularly when you feel you are off course.

Tell the stake president as soon as you think you've made a "blooper."

We all "fall in holes," it's easier to be pulled out before you're up to your neck.

7 The Church
Ward Conference – 4/17/94

Take this talk as a preface to the address to be given by President Tucker. He's going to talk about ministering. No matter what topic may be announced, he'll talk about ministering because that is the stake theme this year.

I would like to say a couple of things about "The Church." Our intonation of "The Church" reveals not an arrogance but an assurance. It is not given as an assertion but as a simple fact. The Church is the structure for the function of ministering, for the good works we do in this sphere. The Church is the form for the content, the kitchen for the preparation of the meal.

The Greek for church is *ekklesia*, as in ecclesiastic. Why invoke the Greek? Or the Hebrew? Or the 19th-century meaning?

Simply because it is the word given by God to his prophets. It is the original text. Notice how copies, like Xeroxed copies, tend to get fuzzy as copies are made of copies. Likewise meanings get corrupted as words are translated and applied in contexts different from those in which they originated. Going back to the original is like getting a fresh look at the document.

Ekklesia comes from ex-kaleo: ex, from (the point of origin) plus a derivation of "to call" (often to a divine vocation) or "to invite." This word is used to translate the Hebrew *qahal*, meaning assembly or congregation — as in Exodus (12:6), which speaks of the whole assembly [the church] of the congregation of Israel.

The church is an assembly of those called. To speak of "The Church" is to speak of those who are called forth. Any other usage is a mistranslation, a corruption of the text, a step toward building idols of our own hand.

Now who is it that calls out; who assembles the people? It can only be the Lord God Himself. (The subject is implicit, unspoken by those called and unseen by the unbeliever.) His sheep recognize the voice of the shepherd. Some chord is struck and it resonates within the heart of the believer.

And who are called out: his sheep, those who follow the shepherd. They are people, people everywhere with very unique personalities and individual differences, but people who share an ear that is receptive to the voice of the shepherd. It includes us who are assembled here today. So what makes us different? The calling!

Called out from where? From the world, from wherever. This is not specified, and once we are in the fold of the shepherd it does not matter from whence we came. Geography does not matter. It is the same whether you have come from the enclave of the Wasatch Front, sunny Florida or smoggy California — it doesn't matter. Social class doesn't matter; doctors and lawyers, taxicab drivers and street-cleaners — it doesn't matter. Age doesn't matter: some are given to see the light in their youth, some in advanced age — it doesn't matter. Recall the parable of the workmen in the fields. All are given the same wage at the end of the day, whether they show up early in the morning or come to the fields in the late afternoon.

We are called from the life we led before: from our ignorance, our pride, sin, backbiting, gossiping, envy, sloth, nastiness, pretensions — whatever sins we have left behind no longer matters, if they are truly left behind. We are called from the world with its lure of glory and fame. We are called from slavish devotion to studies likely to achieve more status in the world. We are called from easy acceptance in our family; some members may understand our life course, but some never quite understand. In this day and age it ain't always cool to be religious.

Called to what? Given the constraints of time, I will just give you the list with references and not try to elaborate. We are called to repentance (Matt. 9:13), to Himself (Rom. 8:30), to fellowship with His Son (1 Cor. 1:9), to peace (1 Cor. 7:15), to freedom (Gal. 5:13), to his kingdom and glory (1 Thes. 2:12), to eternal life (1 Tim. 6:12), to light (1 Pet. 2:9).

We mouth the words, but none of us really has a clue what we are saying. To speak of anything beyond a temporal experience is a statement of faith and hope.

Ekklesia, the assembly of those called forth; we're here together. We come together, today in ward conference. Recently we have assembled in stake conference and general conference.

The local church is the same as the church on any other level. The local assembly is the same as the universal church. Not like, similar to, but the same as. This assembly is the Church restored in these the latter-days. We await the glory of the coming of the Lord.

The Church is right here and now. Not next Sunday, nor in Jackson County. We are together in this room in this moment.

We are in the heaven currently given us. Look around. See the glory of the Lord in the radiance of faces. We are the Church, the assembly. We are called out. May our lives show it! I pray.

Building Zion

Mormon church governance on the local level is characterized by heavenly ideals and homespun practices. The role of the bishop includes pastoral direction to the lay leaders in his ward.

8 Reflections on leadership
Leadership dinner – 10/2/94

The starting point for considering our work in the Church is to always remember that we are doing the work of the Lord. It follows that we should seek His will and His guidance, and call constantly upon Him for help. If we are not building His kingdom, we just have another social club or another public-service association. In church service we ought always to be seeking to act according to His way. This means we ought always to be striving to discover His will. The kicker is that His will is not explicitly and fully written down in any handbook or manual. If you are like me, you are often wondering exactly what is His will. I hold that this lack of explicit direction is purposeful. The will of God remains obscure precisely so we must labor constantly to discover Him. And in this labor we strive to ascertain what God would have for His people, and we yearn for the sense of His grandeur and loving-kindness.

Never forget basic priorities: people count more than programs. Whenever you face a choice between addressing an individual need and "getting the job done," I admonish you to tend to the person. For example, your marriage counts more than your church calling. Whenever you face a choice of sitting in another preparation meeting or relieving your spouse of sitting with a sick child, I hope to not see your face at the meeting. A side note: personally I don't consider your offer to hold your child on your lap during the Final Four basketball games to count under the relief of-spouse clause.

A word about your calling. Note that we speak of our "calling," not our office or position. We are "called" to perform a service in the work of the Lord. But you have, no doubt, noted, often I trust with frustration, that your calling is not explicitly spelled out in detail. This lack of specificity is not necessarily an oversight. It is left for you to ascertain exactly what your calling is. And also what your calling is not. You are to fulfill and to expand your calling, but you are not to take on what is not yours to do. Prayerfully seek to learn the realm in which you may act at your own discretion. Learn when you can say no, when you hold that your available manpower or your budget is insufficient to someone's expectations. Remember that it is your calling. It is for you to ascertain what to do at this specific time and place. In six or 20 years from now when you are a bishop, you will encounter different circumstances, different personalities and different needs.

I hope you will remain mindful of the greater good. One of the geniuses of the Mormon church leadership structure is that members are given a specific calling, which they then tend to "own." That is, they have a personal investment in seeing fulfillment of the programs under their direction. So it often takes a conscious effort to remember that any calling is temporary and somewhat arbitrary. You might consider your calling as your part in a theater play. You are to stay "in role" while on stage, but the role does not define the totality of your person nor of your abilities.

And you may shortly be playing a different role under a different director — unless you are a "johnny-one-note" hack performer.

I would offer a couple of thoughts about the rules and directives under which you operate. The Church has issued instruction manuals for many church positions. The controlling one for the priesthood leadership in the ward is the Bishop's Handbook. I find this a wondrous document, a model of instruction and guidance. It combines general principles of church administration with pointed details while maintaining a wondrous sphere of individual discretion. I have come to think of the Handbook as combining equal parts of inspiration, common sense and "the Mormon way." My experience is that if a person experienced in the Mormon tradition uses his own practical common sense tempered by his prayerful insights, he will come to the course of action laid down in the Handbook.

I offer my take on "rules." Rules are made to be broken, but only when you know the basis for them. My advice is never to break a dictate in any of the church instruction manuals because you decide "this doesn't make any sense." The occasion to alter set proscriptions is when you have full cognizance of why a given rule has been set down and you have full confidence that the persons writing the proscription would approve of your exception if they were aware of the particulars facing you. In this regard, indulge me in an anecdote. In my fourth year of college I wanted to arrange my courses to spend extra time writing my college thesis and to take a course not clearly allowed by the complex rules designed to balance general education with concentration in a particular subject. I studied the official handbook, marshaled my arguments for my case, and with apprehension made an appointment with the associate head of the department who had the determining word in this matter. I sat down with Everett Mendelsohn, laid out my proposal and my arguments, and concluded by saying that perhaps in this particular situation an exception to the rules might be needed. I have a vivid recollection of his leaning back in his chair and an exact memory of his words: "An exception, eh? That's what administrators are for." He had a wisdom and a sense of administration. As a sad incidental note, in the decades since I have never encountered another governmental bureaucrat or business official who voiced such a sentiment.

Two thoughts about your church "service." For your reflection I offer a pithy saying from the Jewish tradition: "Don't be pious at the water-bearer's expense!" This saying emerges from the prescription to wash before certain ceremonial functions. In its practice, more thorough washing has come to signify more concern about performing the function with dedication and thoroughness. You show the level of your piety by the thoroughness of your hand-washing: it's good to wash your hands once; it's better to wash your hands repeatedly; it's best to wash your hands repeatedly using a copious amount of water. But here's the kicker: the water used has to be brought up from the river by the water-bearer.

The second thought: serve with joy. If you don't find true joy in what you are doing, I submit that perhaps you should not be doing it. If preparing a lesson or a talk is a burden, something is amiss. If fulfilling a church service is not joyful, don't do it – or repent! That is, ascertain what prevents such service from being a joy, and change it!

Finally, I ask you to respect one another's callings. Learn the extent and bounds of your calling in the ward. Fill the extent of your calling, but give care not to intrude into the realm of what someone else has been called to do. Remember, whenever you step in to change or override what someone else had done or decided, you undermine their work. It may well be true that your decisions are better than their decisions. But you have to weigh the relative importance: an improvement in a particular project verses the experience and self-confidence of the person making, in your mind, an inferior decision. I urge you to let others learn. And it is, alas, true that we mortals learn best through our mistakes and mishaps

Finally, reflect upon how frequently you make requests of people compared to how often you compliment and thank people for their work. Here I suggest my one quantitatively measurable goal. Strive to have the number of compliments, your "thank you for a job well done" or at least your "thank you for a noble effort" be greater than the number of your requests for someone to take on a job.

9 Pattern your life ... the model of a community
Ward Conference – 4/09/95

The theme for this conference is "Pattern your life after the Master." The concept of "pattern" involves the models we emulate and the model we present. This is a concern of each individual, and also of our communal response and responsibility. I shall speak of models, both individual and communal, and invite your reflection upon the particular applicability of such models in your life.

Today, rather than talk of principles or quote scripture, I shall tell you a couple of stories. I'll tell you of a village in a time that is no more — except as time is eternal, and the village is a community that we are charged to build, even here and now, an outpost of Zion.

I can picture the lanky frame of Lew Munk in front of his class tutoring rough-hewn country lads with callouses on their hands and (some would say) in their heads. He taught me English for four years, and some lessons about life that have lasted forty years. I can picture the gym of the school that doubled as an assembly hall in this town of under 500 people nestled on the creek that brought water and life to the high mountain plains. I've played basketball in that gym. I would share these pictures with you, and let you envision the model this picture suggest.

I shall use words from Darwin Hayes, who retired this spring from the English department at B.Y.U. They might just as well be the words of Ed Geary, Mardin Clark, or David Wright. It's just that I can better picture Darwin and his particular world.

I can picture the structure that Darwin, as a boy, called home. It is a 8 by 10 foot structure with exposed upright 2 x

4's covered by rough-sawed boards inside an inside-out granary sited on Big Creek. I've caught fish from the waters of that creek.

Let me introduce Darwin Hayes. Picture him as a 5-year-old under mounds of home-made quilts watching the shimmer of a red-hot cast-iron cookstove in the middle of that 8 by 10 foot granary while the wind roared around the uninsulated boards at forty degrees below zero.

In the Spring of 1935, Darwin's father is away from home looking for work. His mother feeds the family on milk from their single cow, supplemented by yellow cornmeal and split peas received through the WPA assistance program. Then the cow dries up and the tin of cornmeal is empty. The family eats nothing but split peas for several days.

Hear Darwin's voice.

"I reached a point where I could no longer stomach split peas. I told my mother that I was ready to die and would eat no more. She pulled me close to her, told me she was sorry, that we had to keep eating, and asked me to take my little brother down the creek to see if we could find some fish. That morning the water-master had diverted the water from smaller irrigation channels back into Big Creek, and in the small pools in those smaller streams we found several fish which we caught with our hands. Mother, in the meantime, had found growing in the abandoned corral a small patch of pigweed, a green much like spinach but milder when cooked. I have always counted that meal providential. Ritually, now sixty years later, I nourish a small patch of pigweed each spring in my garden, enough for a single meal, a reminder of having hungered."

There were others who hungered. When the hobos bumming rides on the Union Pacific freight trains came to the door, this mother never invited them into the house where she had gathered her children (though her husband would when he was in town), but she always fed them, sometimes slices of her homemade bread spread with homemade butter and wild chokecherry jelly, sometimes a glass of milk, sometimes nothing more than a cup of creek water. As a child, Darwin wondered how the vagrants knew to walk two miles east from the railroad tracks, then go through the pasture and the corral past the big barn to the granary which housed a woman with children who would always feed a beggar. He remembers his mother's comment about them: "You never know who they might be."

Hear Darwin's voice again.

"My mother was representative of all mothers in that community. It was a safe community of doors without locks, of people trusting, respecting, looking out for one another, working together, sharing what little they had. I know of no child there of my generation who ever ran away from home. It was a community where youth were nurtured for the roles they would assume as adults. Those values were simple, but profound in their influence. First was that education was essential. Every child who hadn't learned to read at home before starting school learned to read well in the first grade. It was unthinkable that we would not do our homework, and we had homework every night.

"Other essential values were compassion, kindness, decency, honesty, integrity. And children learned to value the underdog. The grade school principal played softball with the students at recess and noon hour, and often suspended school until those not adept at hitting a ball not only hit the ball but scored a run. Sometimes a ball game lasted all afternoon."

Lew Munk taught English in that school. One of his sons went to Harvard College on scholarship and now works in the Treasury office once occupied by Alexander

Hamilton. One of his daughters married a sheep-rancher from Cokeville, Wyoming. Of the two, I think his daughter's children had benefit of a more supportive environment.

Hear Darwin's voice about how Lew Munk taught:

"He would send us into the community to collect samples of spoken language that violated the principles he had taught. We attended seriously to the speech of our elders, recording their 'errors' on 3x5 cards — at church, in the store, in public and private activity. Then once a week we would examine our collecting. He would begin class by asking who the most brilliant people in our community were — one week, it would be the most compassionate; another, the most articulate; another, the most inventive. We knew them: we knew that Joe Bee was a mechanical genius, that Roy Robinson was the most persuasive public speaker, that Aunt Maggie King genuinely cared about each of us. We discussed all the town's people in detail. We knew everyone and knew their strengths and their lack of formal schooling. Then Mr. Munk would stop. 'How did I get off on that? You had an assignment for today. What did you find as you listened to the way people use language?' he would say.

"On the board we would list the errors we had collected. Then he would ask us to write the corrections beside the errors, and we would discuss what the errors told us about persons who use language that way. In our innocence and ignorance, at first, we would respond with stereotypes—that such speakers were not very intelligent, or not very good, or not very... whatever. Then he would have us write the names of our sources for each error. And suddenly, he would seem to notice something. 'Wait a minute,' he would say. 'Didn't you just say these people were our village's best. Is there a contradiction here? Make up your minds.'

"He led us to know that one's language does not reflect intelligence or morality or goodness. None of us ever disparaged our elders, or others, for their use of language after that. Our elders were our heroes and our models in community conduct. We looked to them for wisdom."

Allow me one final story from Darwin.

"I remember an incident when I was in fifth grade. Just after the noon hour, the county sheriff, with parents of two boys and the grandfather of another, arrived at school in the sheriff's car. Within a few minutes, Mr. Nielsen, the principal, called five boys from the classroom and shortly thereafter, called all students to gather in the gym. He introduced the sheriff and told us he was visiting the school on official business. The sheriff then explained: during the night, Mr. Hess's service station had been entered, the place had been messed up, and many items had been stolen. Some of the things taken had been recovered; the thieves, whom he named, had been arrested and would not be attending school the rest of that day or the next, since they would have to appear before the judge at the county courthouse in Paris. Then the sheriff and his party left, with our classmates in tow. Mr. Nielsen asked us to return to our classes and to our work."

"That event affected the community profoundly: the wrong doers and their act were made known. So was the judge's decision: the next afternoon the sheriff informed our teacher, who informed us, that the boys were to make full restitution, pay a fine, and were to remain on probation under parental supervision for a specified time. We were asked not to ridicule the boys since they had been appropriately judged. They were to remain part of us. And together we must get on with our studies and with doing that which was right. Neither those boys nor any of the rest of us ever ran afoul of the law again."

A good story doesn't need a moral tacked on the end. I'll not do so.

May God bless those who have served as our models. May God bless us in our striving. May God bless our biological and spiritual children, for generations to come.

I say this in the name of Jesus Christ, the Master, after whom we all pattern our lives, individually and as a community committed to Him and to the building of His kingdom. Amen.

10 To bring our brethren again to thee
Ward Conference – 1/10/99

"Behold, O Lord, their souls are precious... give unto us, O Lord, power and wisdom that we may bring these, our brethren, again unto thee."

Turn to Alma, chapter 31, so we may ponder together the context of our stake theme for the coming year. On this theme, I cannot do better than direct your attention to the Word itself.

Alma receives news that a group led by Zoram are perverting the ways of the Lord. These people have split off from the Nephites, that is, they had accepted God, but they have fallen. Specifically they no longer keep the commandments and laws. They do not live their faith, for example, they do not pray daily.

They worship their own way. They gather on a day "they did call the day of the Lord." Each person would elevate himself — literally. They had a stylized prayer. They addressed God as an eternal spirit, they gave thanks unto God for specific benefits: that they had been separated; that they did not believe the foolish traditions; that they were chosen; that they had not need for a hope in Christ; that they were saved and others were damned to hell.

Their life practice was to speak of God only when assembled, and otherwise to live with their hearts set upon gold and fine goods, upon the vain things of the world.

Hence you can recognize the need to bring me again to the Lord when you see me do the following:

* I separate myself, saying, "I live up on the hill and you in the valley;" "I'm rich (in whatever way) and you're poor;" "I know and you don't know;" "I am saved and you are not."

* I make my religion a matter of public show while ignoring my daily prayers and other private religious practices.

* I am content in my understanding of God's inscrutable ways, that is, I consider my current knowledge of the intangible to be sufficient, and perceive no need to live in the hope of the redemption of Christ.

How will you bring me again to the Lord? If you follow the model of Alma, you will have the following response.

* You will recognize the virtue of the word of God is more powerful than the sword, or anything else.

* You will be sick at heart at my iniquity and pained in your soul at my wickedness.

* You will pray for strength to suffer in patience, for comfort, and for success in your endeavors.

If you follow the model of Alma, you will follow this course of action: First, turn to God to ascertain the way you should pursue; do not rely upon your own devices, upon your own knowledge, calculations, and cleverness. Second, recognize that all souls are precious; these are our brethren, whatever their beliefs and practices, however repugnant and odiferous we find them, even if they are University of Utah fans, born-agains, or Democrats — or, Heaven forbid, all three! Third, ask God for power and wisdom. True power and wisdom comes to us from God.

If we follow the recorded precedent in Alma, we will set upon our task without concern for our own needs, not even for the basics of food, drink, and clothing. And our afflictions in the work will be "swallowed up in the joy of Christ."

Let us live in daily prayer to God for His power and wisdom. Precious souls lie in balance. My soul needs your prayers. Pray to keep me, and all of us, in the Word of God. Amen.

11 What we make of it
Sacrament Meeting – 7/25/99

Good help is hard to hire nowadays. I'm glad we do not have to pay for church service. We couldn't afford the help. There is no earthly currency for the qualities we are most in need of: faithfulness, devotion, long-suffering, slowness to judgment, attention to the details that bring no fame nor glory.

I would personally, and publicly, welcome Brother Barlow into the bishopric. Not that the choice was hard. He was the only face in the congregation with a goatee. We gave Brother Cameron six years, but he either couldn't or wouldn't grow a beard. In this church, everyone may exercise his or her free agency, but every action does have its consequence.

I would personally, and publicly, give acknowledgment to Brother Cameron — and to all the other members who have and do serve in this ward. For me, rules of good management are like the rules of etiquette my mother taught me; just because I don't follow them is not evidence that I am not aware of them. I am aware that rules of good management dictate feedback loops: you assign a task, make a notation in your tickler file, and then call the person in to have a report on when and how the task was done. For me, it has been a personal delight that when Brother Cameron said, "I'll take care of that," and it was taken care of. "I'll do it," and it is done! This is characteristic of so many who make the functional operation of the ward as smooth as it is. "I'll have the sacrament table prepared," and it is. "I'll have music prepared," and it is. "I'll see that the tithing receipts are counted and deposited," and they are. "I'll see that the chapel is cleaned up," and it is. "I'll see that the primary children have a lesson," and they do. "I'll see that the nursery has snacks," and it does. "I'll see that six people are at the temple for a sealing session," and they are. "I'll see that the Relief Society room is prepared," and it is. I could go on and on.

These are illustrations of a general principle. I have a bias that our corner of the kingdom is what we make of it. I trust that the Lord oversees the building of the kingdom, and has a vibrant interest in the smallest detail. And with this I have supposed that the Lord purposefully restrains Himself so that we can make our own lives. My conceptualization of the ward is that we organize ourselves. The function of the bishopric, and the entire ward leadership, is to recognize the organization that you ask for and to provide it without undue delay or hassle. That principle, applied to this ward, means if you have good leadership, congratulations! You have gotten what you deserve. If ward leadership, on whatever level, is less than what you desire, I submit that your question ought to be: "What am I to do to see the desire of my heart is actualized?" What you desire is what you get; what you receive is intrinsically related to what you contribute.

Your coming into this ward is good. Your staying in this ward is good. Your leaving is also good — because the saints of another ward have need of you, and you have need of what your encounter with them will bring. May the Lord bless our efforts, all of them. Each of us has a critical role, and none is to be judged against another. May all of our efforts be an anthem to the Lord and a blessing to us, our progenitors and our posterity.

I pray this in the name of Jesus Christ, the architect of His Church and Lord of His Kingdom. Amen.

Living the Gospel

The bishop is to reinforce members' commitment to living the Gospel principles. He tries to inspire and to encourage members to make theological principles an intrinsic part of their daily lives.

12 Meaning of temple work
Sacrament Meeting – 8/28/94

Today I'm the concluding speaker, but that does not mean I get the last word. You do! Because what you do in your daily life after all these words are said determines the worth of our gathering together today.

My topic today is the meaning of temple work. Meaning grows out of experience. Meaning comes after you do something, not when you just contemplate it. For example, you can contemplate what it would be like being married, but you really don't know what marriage is about until it is too late. The same holds for going to college, taking on a church calling, or raising children. This generalization applies particularly in raising children.

Meaning cannot be determined in advance of the experience from which it comes. It has to be revealed, i.e. uncovered. So meaning, viewed in this light, is a personal matter and largely undefinable.

Meaning is an individual matter and is as varied as our individual life experiences. Two of us may be involved in the same activity but take away different experiences. And for each of us even the same act may have different meanings at different times. For example, my washing the dishes may be assuming my fair share of housework (or making the occasional pretense of doing so), my compulsive need for tidiness, or my deciding to clean up the kitchen before Barbara comes home from a three-day trip—giving the appearance that I have kept it that way the entire time she was gone.

This introduction is my way of acknowledging that many of us may have many different kinds of experience in the temple. And our own experiences may vary with time. Having said this, I'll offer four common meanings to temple attendance.

First, this is a place and time to be in God's House. For this alone, you might say that you could go into the forest or scale a mountain peak, and there bask in the glory of God's handiwork and imbibe a sense of his grandeur and love. Many people do, and this, too, has its place, for all of the earth is the Lord's. Unique to the temple is that it is a space specifically dedicated to the Lord. It is set apart and reserved for the purpose of our encountering the Lord and his greatness and goodness. While we can enjoy a feast on our usual plastic plates, we know that special occasions call for bringing out the special china.

Second, in the temple we join in fellowship of the saints for a focused purpose. The setting promotes our leaving the worries and concerns of the world behind, to appreciate better the eternal sphere in which we live, even while confined here in a puny body in time and space. Here we are all alike before God. All differences of social status, education, and earthly wealth are removed. The setting reminds us that we are all children of God, none favored over another in God's love and mercy. This is manifest, for example, by all dressing in simple white. Here today, you may reflect upon the symbolism. Our temple clothes are more than Joseph's coveted coat of many colors. White is the sum of all color. Within the walls of the temple we wear the sum of all experience, all contemplation, all hopes and all desires.

Third, in the temple we focus upon learning the unfolding of God's plan. We are explicitly invited to reflect upon the purpose of creation, our place in it, for what we are destined, and how we might free our life of the distractions from our most important goals. Such instruction involves an incomprehensible condensation. Imagine a scholar trying to reduce 50 years of study into a single one-hour lecture. In temple instruction, the Lord condenses the totality of human existence down to one short script.

Finally, participation in temple service allows us to make and renew our covenants with God. You could think of temple ordinances as an extension of your baptismal covenants. What is implicit in baptism is given more explicitly in the temple.

I would offer one word of friendly caution. The world is open to the influence of the Adversary, and the Adversary makes a concerted effort to discredit, distort, and demean everything sacred in an ongoing attempt to remove mortals from God's influence and power. So it is logical that special effort would be put into distorting temple service and ceremonies. If you find yourself bothered by anything you hear or read about the temple, please call Joe Vance for an appointment to sit down and talk with me. I would welcome hearing your concerns. If you bring in something new to my ears, I'll thank you for expanding my life experience. The basic problem is that some things said about temple service are plain wrong, and some things are accurate but taken out of context. Placed in their proper context some things are not only understandable, but appear essential.

God's ways are greater than our ways. Your life will be easier when you believe that.

I'm here to urge explicitly your attendance at the temple. I am not here to pass judgment upon anyone who is not attending the temple regularly. Everyone has this own life circumstances and everyone has his own reasons. My paternal grandfather spent the greater part of the last third of his life in the Salt Lake City Temple. Family lore has it that at his death he had done more sealings than anyone else in the Church. For the first two-thirds of his life, he was hardly ever found in the temple. His life circumstances were not conducive to being in the temple. For all things there is a season.

Ask yourself if in this season you would live better by being in the temple more often. If so, I pray that you may find the motivation and means to be there.

13 Follow the prophet
Sacrament Meeting – 11/03/96

This October, Barbara and I attended General Conference. This is the first time in my life that I have done so. It was a cultural experience. The one talk by President Hinckley was worth the price of admission. I recommend his talk to you, found in the November *Ensign*, page 68 and 69.

I draw your attention to a half dozen sentences near the end of that talk.

"Some years ago President Benson delivered a message to the women of the Church. He encouraged them to leave their employment and give their individual time to their children. I sustain the position which he took.

"Nevertheless, I recognize, as he recognized, that there are some women (it has become very many in fact) who have to work to provide for the needs of their families. To you I say, do the very best you can."

Note the conclusion. On a weighty, and often contentious matter, what is the deliberate advice of the Prophet? "Do the very best you can." When all is said and done, his summary statement is, "Do the very best you can."

Shortly after President Benson delivered the message mentioned by President Hinckley, I was visiting in the Wasatch Front. It was sad to hear the bickering. Women not working outside the home took it upon themselves to chastise their sisters who did. Working women justified their work, or deprecated any and all they saw criticizing them for their employment outside the home.

Listen carefully to President Hinckley's reference to President Benson: "I recognize, as he recognized, that there are some women ... who have to work... ." President

Hinckley recognizes individual needs, and he says that President Benson recognized these individual needs. President Hinckley's elaboration is embedded in President Benson's address. I suppose that in a few years yet another prophet will have to make explicit what President Hinckley is saying this year.

Consider the nature of the prophet. Prophet, in its original Hebrew form, *navi*, means nothing other than "the word of the Lord comes to you." The Lord's word may be uttered by the head of the Church, or it may come as a still voice to your heart. Both are equally the word of the prophet. Both convey the same message. Listen to the prophet, and hearken to the word of the Lord.

If you heard of President Benson's injunction and did not hear the recognition that you are to do the very best you can, then you did not truly hear the word of the prophet. If you heard President Hinckley's address and did not hear true concern for your salvation and for the well-being of future generations, then you did not truly hear the word of the prophet. The still small voice guiding you says the same as the spokesman for the Church, the man whom we sustain as prophet, seer, and revelator. And hear the two final sentences from this spokesman.

"Many of you spend much time on your knees speaking with your Father in Heaven, with tears running down your cheeks. Please know that we also pray for you."

This I say in the name of Jesus Christ, amen.

14 Laws and commandments of the gospel
Sacrament Meeting – 11/24/96

I thank [the previous two speakers] for their thoughts and for the spirit in which they are given. Also for their taking time I otherwise might use. I'm relatively safe for the first eight minutes, then I run the risk of getting dangerous. I would preface my remarks with the observation that a bishop may encourage and support, but he is not empowered to proclaim doctrine. So please take encouragement and support, but feel free to disregard anything not recognizable as Mormon doctrine.

Today I would address what it means to be a good Mormon, or how to live as a human, as a Mensch, in the Mormon context. What are we to do with our lives? How am I to live?

For my text today I would take the temple recommend interview. A temple recommend interview could be done with a two-sentence exchange. Bishop: "Are you still worthy to participate in temple ordinances?" Ward member: "Yes!" — or "No!" So why the questions? You might consider this an annual self-examination of how you live, of how you are doing as a Mormon Mensch.

I will mention items briefly rather than expound on what most of you already know. I'd ask you to take out a pencil or pen, and make a note on the program if I allude to something that is not clear. Then take it up with your visiting teachers when they come by. Or phone your home teachers and invite them to come by. Or raise a question in Sunday School class. Or ask me what I meant, or what I intended to mean.

The temple recommend interview asks about three specific Mormon practices.

1. Are you a full-tithe payer? In other words, do you return to the Lord 10% of your annual increase? (Incidentally, I would note annual tithing-settling is coming up; I encourage all to attend.)

2. Do you keep the Word of Wisdom? At its most superficial level this means to avoid alcohol, tobacco, illegal drugs, coffee, and black tea.

3. Do you live the law of chastity? Mormons are expected to have no sexual intimacy outside of the marriage covenant.

There is inquiry into three specific interpersonal practices. I can imagine such an inquiry could be made into 30 practices, or for that matter 300. I suspect these three are mentioned precisely because they are not always observed.

1. Is your conduct in relation to members of your family in harmony with teachings of the Church? At the very least, this means no abuse of any kind. No physical abuse, no sexual abuse, no verbal threatening, no psychological intimidation.

2. If you have been divorced or separated, are you meeting financial and other legal obligations? The fact of a divorce does not erase contractual and moral obligation to ex-spouse and children.

3. Are you honest in your dealings with your fellowman? You can't be a good Mormon and run a scam.

The list of questions about religious beliefs is remarkably short.

1. Do you have a testimony of God the Eternal Father, Jesus Christ, and the Holy Ghost?

2. Do you have a testimony of the atonement of Christ and his role as Savior and Redeemer?

3. Do you have a testimony of the restoration of the gospel in these days?

Note this is not just a question of mere belief. It is an inquiry into your spiritual experience, what you have lived and hence can give testimony of.

Then there are questions about your religious practice — which I shall paraphrase here.

1. Do you sustain recognized Church authorities?

2. Do you not subscribe to heterodox teachings or practices or support those who do?

3. Do you presume to hide sins or misdeeds that should have been resolved, but have not been? Confession and repentance erases sin. Though they be as red as scarlet, they may become as white as snow. But pretending to hide sin is not compatible with being a good Mormon.

4. Do you strive to keep covenants made, attend sacrament meetings, (and for men, priesthood meetings)? Note this question is "Do you strive to..." Other matters are black and white. Either you pay a full tithe or not. Either you keep the Word of Wisdom as operationally defined or not. But here the question is "Do you strive to..." If you are not at church because you are at home with a sick spouse, or tending children, or having to work, you are to ask yourself, "Whatever I am doing, am I striving to keep my covenants and to attend sacrament meetings, etc."

Finally, "Do you keep your life in harmony with the laws and commandments of the gospel?" In harmony with the gospel, not the Church, priesthood or church handbook.

I would elaborate on the meaning of "laws and commandments of the gospel." Gospel in the New Testament is *evangelium*, the "good news." The equivalent Hebrew word is *besar*, which means good news, tidings, the message, or bearer of the message. However, if you look up *b-s-r*, in a Hebrew Bible, you will find it is much more often translated as "flesh," yes, "flesh." So the question is: do you live in harmony with the laws and commandments of the flesh?

Flesh is the material form which God bestows by means of His creation. Flesh is the Good News of Jesus appearing as a mortal. In his appearance on the American continent the resurrected Jesus says: "Behold I have given unto you my gospel, and this is the gospel which I have given unto you — that I came into the world to do the will of my Father, because my Father sent me." (3 Nephi 27:13) The gospel is Jesus coming into the world to do the will of God the Father. The gospel is likewise our soul being clothed in flesh in the world, doing the will of our Father. Living the gospel is living in accord with what we intrinsically know is right, what our inner self says: "That's the right thing." It is not "conventional wisdom," not what "everyone is doing," not what some external authority tells us to do. It is doing what our inner self tells us is the right thing to do. This is not doing what feels good, not what comes easily, nor not necessarily what we want for ourselves. It is doing what is right.

I surmise God designed creation as He did in order to allow us to connect with the Divine within — given that each of us is made in the image of God. Such a design allows us to act from our own volition, to do much good without being commanded by another.

Take one practical example: visiting teaching. Visiting teachers are assigned by the Relief Society president to "look after" designated sisters. When a sister is in need, the first question is "Who is her visiting teacher?" You may not appropriate the status of a visiting teacher. You can't claim on your own: "I am the visiting teacher for Sister Smith," for this is an assignment. But you can look after Sister Smith without a designated assignment or calling. You can look around the chapel and ask, "Who's not here, and should I do something about this? Is someone in premature labor? Or ill? Or burdened with unshared cares?" You can pick up the telephone when someone comes into your mind inexplicably and you get that inner sense that you ought to call. Now, you don't foist yourself onto an unwilling recipient, but you can always act as a "good friend," as a real Mensch.

To do good for a reward is a commercial transaction. You do X-good and you get Y-reward. Scripture has a harsh word for people who make such calculations. They are called "money-changers." Now money-changers are useful in the commercial arena, but they do not belong in that sphere where God lives in Zion. Jesus does not chastise nor kill the money-changers, he simply drives them from His temple.

I rejoice in the good that you do. I respect and love you for it. This I say in the name of Jesus Christ.

15 The duties of members
Ward Conference – 3/23/97

It is my observation that a Mormon conference has two essential components. One is to hear something like an annual report. My assignment is to address the question, "How are we doing?" In this regard, I think back on the visiting professor at my college who returned to Europe without turning in his grades. Students couldn't graduate without grades, so a hurried telegram was sent to Paris: "Wire grades by return post." The next day came a ten-word telegram in return: "I enjoyed the class. Stop. Give all students A's. Stop." This is my report: "I've enjoyed the ward. Period. Give all members A's. Stop."

In particular I enjoy the willingness of members to accept callings, to define them, to expand them, and to serve in them with joy. I enjoy the initiative of ward members: doing good without a formal calling, seeing a need, stepping up, and offering a hand. I enjoy seeing the growth of members in Christ, starting with Primary. You ought to see the front row in Primary; they are so much more mature since they graduated from the nursery.

The second essential part of a Mormon conference is to get a sermon so you can go home and feel guilty about what you're not doing. Now, I do not want you to go home and feel guilty about the little things. I want you to save your guilt for a worthwhile cause.

I don't want you to feel guilty when the couple with three kids in front of you scurries out leaving a mess of papers and crumbs — which you then walk away from. I do not want you to feel guilty about leaving it; just pick it up!

I don't want you to feel guilty about nit-picking the bishop and his two counselors. They probably deserve it, and if they're innocent of this particular complaint, they have probably done something else just as egregious, or left something else undone. This license, please note, does not extend to other teachers and leaders in the ward. We're a lay-church, and everyone's trying to do their best. It might be different than your best, but it's their turn to fulfill their calling in their way. So please, just pick on the bishopric.

I don't want you to feel guilty for incidental lapses in desired activities:

* for picking up some baby formula at the store on Sunday evening;

* for nodding off in a Sacrament Meeting talk that has been extended beyond its content;

* for skipping out of Sunday School class to socialize and do necessary business in the foyer;

* for not getting to the temple as often as you think you should.

I am not urging such lapses as a desirable norm, but don't go home from this meeting feeling guilty about them.

Above all, I don't want you to feel guilty about your rotten attitude. If you are like me, you have your moments when faith is lacking, moments of irritation at your spouse, times when you'd like to string up your kids by their toes. You get frustrated at the stupidities done in the church with self-righteous overtones; you doubt your own testimony; you're fed up with yourself, and are angry with God. Don't worry about God. Taking on unwarranted anger is part of His job description. He knows what to do about it, how to turn it to His glory. God is more accepting of us than we are of ourselves. The critical thing is to engage yourself in a discussion with God.

So what should you feel guilty about? You ought to feel guilty about not doing your duty. And what is your duty? Let everyone turn to D&C 20:68-69.

68: "The duty of the members... [is] to manifest... before the church... by a godly walk and conversation... that there may be works and faith agreeable to the holy scripture — walking in holiness before the Lord."

Note that duty is singular. One overriding all-comprehensive duty. If you are going to go home and feel guilty, then let your guilt be that your walk and talk is not holy before the Lord. One thing is asked of members: be holy in your walk; let Christ live in you; be His; be a Christian.

The most current expression of this duty is given by President Hinckley in his October, 1996 conference address. He is talking about our obligation to the fatherless and widows, and cites a letter in which expected behavior is laid out. This is what he passes on, in an approving fashion, from a sister in need who was sustained by the saints around her.

"We were always met with loving hearts and warm handshakes. The Christlike attitude of the stake and our ward has helped us through trials we never imagined possible." In summary, President Hinckley talks of "a host of ward members who are helpful without being intrusive."

I commend both sides of this advice to you. On the one side, be helpful: reach out and give a hand. On the other side, do not be intrusive. Curtail your personal curiosity why someone is doing or not doing something. Do not ask overly personal questions. If particular information is not volunteered, then you do not need to know. You are to have a loving heart and a warm handshake, not detailed facts needed to pass critical judgment.

I would sum up my thoughts by relating an apocryphal story; apocryphal means a story so good that it had to be made up. The disciple John, John the Beloved, as an old man was visiting a distant branch of the church — probably in the southern part of North Seattle. He was helped to the stand to share with the assembled saints all that he had learned from being at the side of the Savior. He stood at the pulpit, said: "Children, love one another," and he sat down. The local bishop, thinking he was too weak to stand, lent him a cane, and helped him back to the stand. John spoke out: "Children, love one another," and he sat down. The bishop, thinking the aged John was too weak to support himself, this time stood at his side. John said: "Children, love one another. That is all there is to be said," and he sat down.

So, my children, in the name of Jesus Christ, I tell you, love one another. That is all there is to be said.

16 Two kinds of cookies; two sets of books
Sacrament Meeting – 11/28/99

[To the Primary children assembled at the front of the chapel:]

What holiday did we just celebrate?
Why is it called Thanksgiving?
How does eating a turkey give thanks?
What does it mean to give thanks?

I guess that some questions have answers and some questions are there just to think about.

Now I want to return thanks to you. At the Primary program Chi Chi handed me a gift from all of you. It is this "pot of flowers," with one of your faces in the middle of each flower. That is a very nice thing you gave me. Now I want to give something back. Here are a couple of plates stacked with home-baked cookies. Everyone take one. Keep it until you get back in your seats. Put off eating it as long as you are able. If you do eat it before I finish talking, try not to leave crumbs on the carpet.

Now I want to talk with you a minute about these cookies. I think I notice something. Some of the cookies were nice golden brown ones. You took those. And some cookies were black icky burnt stuff. You left those on the plate! How come? Both are prepared from the same material: same flour, same sugar, same chocolate chips. Ah, right on! Some were prepared with careful attention, and some just thrown into the oven and ignored until the smoke started to come out around the oven door.

One last thing. Sometimes I've had moments of resentment at having to give up some of my cookies. Have you ever tried that? When you had to share a toy, or share time with your grandmother with that ungrateful little brother? And, truth be told, most everyone I know has some black thoughts about sharing. Now black thoughts often come out as black deeds, and that's not as nice as a thank-you. But some things in life do come out black — but they can still be used, even if we can't see how.

Here's what you don't know: I'll take these black things back home and feed them to the birds in our back yard. Birds fly in the heavens; they know how to use even black stuff.

Thanks again for the Primary program, and for all you bring to our ward.

It is good that bishops may only minister and tell stories, and are not allowed to formulate doctrine. Else I would bring in my own theology. You see, I have come to the conclusion that the Lord keeps two sets of books. My accountant friends tell me that it is a no-no to keep two sets of books, but I can't shake off the impression that is exactly what the Lord does.

I'll apply this to tithing as an illustration. Tithing settlement comes up this time of year. Money can be counted, so we can use that for an example. Brother Michael Smith, our financial clerk, and I keep track of one set of books. We tally up the individual contributions and make sure it equals the bank deposit. And in annual tithing settlement Brother Smith will reconcile your record of contributions with ours. I'll record your declaration if your tithing contribution is full, or partial, or if you are exempted, i.e., have no income that is to be tithed.

I take what you tell me at face value. I don't see that it's my role to go out of my way to tell you how you should earn your money, how hard you should work to earn more money, nor precisely how you should interpret the revelation given in 1838 that "...my people...shall pay one-tenth of all their interest annually..." (D&C 119:3-4).

Just imagine me in the bishop's office.

"Sister Clark, is this $900 a full tithe? Yes. But you're supposed to be retired! You're working too hard. I'll have your husband talk to you about this."

"Jimmie, is your 9 cents a full tithe? No? Your little sister swallowed a penny! Shall we let your mother worry about that, or just not tell her?"

The bishop's responsibility is to ensure that the church accounts faithfully reflect your records, and that all monies are faithfully deposited. It is your responsibility to tell me if your tithe is full, or partial, or if you are exempt. What you declare is what I record. I'm not planning to go uninvited into the details of your financial arrangements.

I reflect that my father paid tithing on his Social Security payments, and then considered his Social Security withdrawals to already have been tithed. And I know good members who do not consider money withheld from their paycheck to be income, and who plan to later tithe their Social Security payments after they retire.

I reflect that my father usually wrote a check at the end of the year for his annual tithing. That made sense for him, given that most of the family income came in two annual checks: one from the sale of wool in the late spring, and one from the sale of the lambs in the late fall. But I would definitely not recommend semiannual payments for any family living from paycheck to paycheck. It's too easy to fall behind, and there are always unexpected expenses.

I know some students who tithe their loans and stipends, and many who do not. In my days of poverty, I considered my college scholarship as a grant from the gifts of university donors given me to cover expenses and not as income available to me, hence not to be tithed.

I cite these few specifics as a lead-in to my speculation about the Lord's second set of books. My speculation is that the Lord reads our hearts as well as surveys the financial ledger. It's like the compensation that we receive for our church service: the pay is nothing to talk about, but the retirement benefits are out of this world.

My imagination is that the Lord is more concerned about the spirit in which tithing is given than the dollar amount. I imagine that the Lord rejoices in the widow's mite and Jimmie's nine cents. I imagine that He reads our hearts and rejoices when He sees a willing heart, a glad heart, a heart giving in thankful return.

Let me share my understanding of tithes and offerings. Both are free will contributions. Tithes are expected; offerings are encouraged. Mormons customarily contribute 10% of their income to the Church toward building the Kingdom of God, and also make a monthly contribution of the cost of a day's meals for the sick and needy, which funds are administered by the bishops of the Church.

Some people, who can well afford it, make a fast offering contribution of two, or ten times, the cost of a couple of meals. Also many families make regular contributions to the Church Humanitarian Fund, the Missionary Fund, or other special funds.

Personally, even when means are meager, I think it is a good practice to cultivate the habit of giving a small token amount to keep alive your intent to share if and when your financial situation allows greater generosity. For example, our daughter's means are meager, but when she signs her first million dollar acting contract, she states the intent to buy a red Mercedes for her mother and a black Harley-Davidson for her father. (But don't stand waiting in the parking lot to see this.)

To get to the practicalities. Sign up for tithing settlement, review your financial situation, come in ten minutes before your scheduled time to compare records with Brother Michael Smith. Know that for the IRS charitable deductions in 1999, monies have to be deposited in 1999. But the Lord's second set of books are always open, and you may have tithing settlement at any time of the year.

Also, in planning your budget of contributions for the coming year, I would alert you to the fact that our ward may well support another missionary, as we did Elder Bruce Johnson. Among the 80-plus young men whom Bishop Furness has sent out from one of the university wards is a young man whom we may support to the amount of $360 per month for 24 months.

In conclusion, may you see the Lord's blessings. Sometimes they're obvious, and sometimes they're disguised. Just as I thanked the children, I want to thank you. Sorry there's not enough cookies to go around, but I understand the Service and Activities Committee has a nice treat planned on this coming Friday at 6 p.m. at our ward Christmas party.

Personal Worship

Walk With God

While the Mormon church maintains a sturdy institutional control, Mormon doctrine allows extensive variations in individual thought and worship. The following sermons address aspects of members' personal relationships to God and their striving to emulate Him and His teachings in their daily lives.

17 In the year that Uzziah died
Sacrament Meeting - 8/29/93

In the time and place where I first heard (and learned to give) a 2½-minute talk, it was a fixed feature of the 10 o'clock morning Sunday School. Ward members had a sure sense of its proper form and allowable content, but they would have considered talk of a "genre" to be unduly abstract and uppity.

I dedicate this presentation to that culture with its plain ways. Its form is from my childhood Mormon experience. Its content is drawn from my more mature reflections.

"In the year that king Uzziah died I saw also the Lord sitting upon a throne..." (Isaiah 6:1)

"I saw also..." A quaint King James Version phrase, not put into more modern translations, which seems to take the year as a reference point for historical dating. But the original Hebrew has a construction that the old King James translators rendered as "also." The revised King James Version reads "then." I prefer the old rendition, which suggests the association is not just an historical dating but is a profoundly moving personal statement by Isaiah about himself, and about each of us.

Isaiah was a friend, confidant, and counselor of kings. Uzziah was a good king and a dear friend. In the year that Uzziah died, Isaiah was alone, stripped of his friendship and facing years of having to give counsel that would not be taken well. In that year he was alone. In that year of loneliness he *saw also the Lord*. When the Lord's servant was stripped of human companionship, the heavens opened themselves to him and he *saw*. No vague premonition. No hearsay. No subjective inner conviction. Isaiah *saw*!

Each of us have our years when we are left without our best friend. Our spouse dies. Our schoolmates scatter. Our children leave home. Our attachments in this world are broken. We lose people we love, things we esteem, our good opinion of ourselves. In that year we are alone. In this same year, in our grief, our aloneness, our unspoken and unspeakable anguish, we, too, may *see also the Lord*. He is ever mindful of us, and ever close. Our friend may die, but our LORD is ever with us. When our friends are gone, our comforts passed, then in that very year we have possibilities to see what we have never seen before.

18 Your personal relationship with God
Sacrament Meeting, – 10/22/95

The quest to cultivate one's private spirituality is not highlighted in Mormonism. To be sure, the need for a personal testimony is commonly acknowledged, but the practical emphasis is more on communal aspects of worship. Mormons are characterized more by their "activity" than by piety. Yet a longing for a more personal and more meaningful relation with God smolders in many a breast. I would address some aspects of this yearning.

Man, formed from the dust of the earth, became a living soul when the Lord God breathed the breath of life into his nostrils. (Genesis 2:7) The soul of man has origin in the breath of God, and every subsequent breath of man affirms this innate, essential relation to his creator. Each of us lives in this intimate bond to God; to connect to God is nothing other than to live in constant awareness of this bond.

A personal relationship with God is equally available to all. It is not dependent upon sex, age, intelligence, wealth, or place in the organized Church hierarchy. A nine-year-old girl has as ready access to the Lord God as the president of the Church. A socially-marginal dyslexic with sub-normal intelligence can be as close to God as a prominent, intelligent, highly-educated and well-read matron of Mormon society.

A personal relationship with God is a personal matter. It may be reflected in one's outer walk, or it may be completely hidden from view. From my own experience, I reflect upon the immediacy of prayers uttered by the man who had not set foot in the church house for some 30 years. Conversely, I have heard more than one stake president privately bemoan his almost total lack of a sense of walking with God. One's relation with God is hidden from the world. It may even often by hidden from oneself. In your inner being, in the core of your soul, you may already be much closer to the Lord God than you consciously realize. You can never judge another in this matter, and you most likely cannot even judge yourself.

I'll share a couple of introductory thoughts about cultivating your relation to God. First, living with God is different from studying about God. Study about God involves an objective perspective that may accumulate many facts but nevertheless keeps one distant from one's Creator. Living with God does not require accumulation of facts or cultivation of technique. It is a matter of one's being. Living with God begins with who you are. What you do is a derived quality and not a primary characteristic.

Second, a walk with God is a lonely trek. You will start by being driven by urges you cannot explain. Along the way you will not be able to adequately describe your experience. At the end you will have no one with whom you can share the depth of your adventure. If fact, you most likely will see your friends fall away and you may well despair of not ever having a true confidant.

By definition, a walk with God is a personal trek. There is no handbook on how to do it. You cannot single out any other person as a model to follow in all particulars. There are no prescribed rituals or techniques. Your walk with God is singular and therefore unique. To be sure, you can draw upon the insights of others who have gone their way. But if you have a personal relationship with God, it will be like none other.

Now, how to begin. Start with the desire. The desire of the heart may or may not be realized because of external conditions, but the desire counts for itself. A prayer from the heart is answered in its utterance. You may, or may not, see anything change in external circumstances. But be assured that prayer is efficacious; it goes straight to heaven and the recording angels rejoice.

Second, know that the walk begins in the dark and the way becomes lighted as you walk along. In the words of Spencer W. Kimball: "Faith precedes the miracle.." You first do it, then you may see the results of the effort. For example, God shows the power of prayer to those who have been on their knees. The armchair philosopher may speculate about prayer, but he never personally lives in its power. Confirmation comes to the committed; the sceptic is rich in reservations and hence never condescends to being poor in spirit.

Third, look for God's working in your life. Eyes that are open to the working of the Spirit see God's hand. Take God at his word. At the close of each day of creation God says: "It is good," and at the conclusion of creation He says, "It is very good." Live in the assumption that all things coming into your life are for your good. Easy to do in good times and darn hard in what we call bad times. Here we come up against whose definition of good we live with. Mortals judge good and bad by mortal standards; God has a divine standard. When we weigh our life by our standards, we remain in our own mortal plane. When we say, "This too is for my good," (though we don't have a clue why and don't feel it in our narcissistic core) we engage in a struggle to live in the eternal sphere while yet in our mortal existence.

God will draw us to Him. He does this as a good father draws a child to his feet and urges her to walk by herself. He first lifts up the child and steadies her in her first faltering steps. When the child has a measure of equilibrium and a tad of confidence, the father distances himself so the child has a space to walk in order to be again in her father's arms.

The more distant the father, the greater the father's confidence in the toddler's developing skills.

Fourth (and this will be enough for today), thank God constantly. I have never seen a soul wither in disbelief from thanking God too much. Thank Him in general and thank Him in the particulars. Thank Him for your flocks and your fields, for your varied life experiences and the opportunities (experienced as aggravations and bothers by the spiritually blind). Thank Him for hard professors and children crying in the night; thank Him that women and men dedicated to learning require you to stretch your mind and make the most of your academic years. Thank Him you have a child that can call out its needs rather than languish in silence while you sleep in blissful ignorance of a soul entrusted to your care. Thank Him for provisions beyond what you saw need for. What does this mean? I'll share one short story and close.

Corrie ten Boom, the Dutch woman who gave Jews refuge in her attic until she herself was betrayed and interned, lived through her time in a concentration camp, and gave thanks for all of God's graces — except for the fleas in the sleeping quarter which gave no relief from persistent bites and itching. Only after their release did a friend point out that the Nazi guards never entered the sleeping quarters, precisely because they wanted to avoid the fleas. So their beloved Bible was secreted away there, and the women could gather there for hidden reading and mutual solace.

19 The foundation of our life
Sacrament Meeting – 10/9/94

I want to address the foundation of our life, to talk about the spirituality that supports our good works. We admire the pillars of our community and the pillars of our ward. We look up to those who stand tall, who are seen doing good works. We don't see the foundation, but this is what supports the pillars and the entire building.

My elementary knowledge of the construction of foundations is that you dig down below the frost line, pour concrete wider than the intended walls, and then cover it up. This means you dig to a level deeper than where the temperature changes, deeper than the vicissitudes of passing fashion. You prepare a foundation more solid and more wide than that which you expect to be seen. Then you cover over what you have done.

Consider the four sons of Mosiah. All served missions to the Lamanites. Ammon watched the flocks of the king, killed the bad guys, then converted the king's household and ended up riding in his chariot. The mission experience of his brother Aaron was to *begin* expounding the gospel, then to be taken captive, cast into prison and suffer many things until his brothers came to rescue him. Who's to say which brother served a more honorable mission? The record speaks of all having the same foundation. In Alma 17:2-3 we read that they were men of a sound understanding who had searched the scriptures diligently, given themselves to much prayer and fasting.

The hidden foundation is the support of good works throughout the world. The opinions of Mother Teresa are now picked up by the Associated Press. She is "good press" since her good works have come to light. But I know good sisters who have taken the same vows of poverty, do equally good work, but are never given any press coverage. The motivation of these sisters, in the words of Mother Teresa, is to see the image of Christ in every face.

There is a old Jewish tradition that all of creation is sustained by the lives of 36 unknown holy ones. Whenever one passes on or is exposed as a holy one, another takes his place. When they cease to be hidden, they cease to be holy. We can understand that. When we tout ourselves as Christians, we lose something of our Christianity. When we boast of ourselves as Mormons, we lose something of the promise of the restoration of the fullness of all things. There are exactly 36, not more or less. This has its rationale. It is the fullness or completion of six. You scientists and higher mathematical types can figure that out for yourselves: 36 is six times six. The world is created in seven days; we live in the seventh. Six represents all that has proceeded this day, all that God has done in preparation for what we can see. The six times six is the fullness of the foundation of the world. It is our tie to heaven, our unconscious connection to all that God has done before we take charge of the situation. It is this connection that sustains all of creation and prevents it from collapsing like a house of cards.

We cannot see our foundation, but we can see the pillars built upon it. A few examples. We see the freshly pressed white linen cloth covering the sacrament of the Lord's Supper, but do not know who washed and pressed it — much less their motivation in such a service.

There is a woman in the ward you have not seen in the church building for the past year. But every month I see her tithing check. She is at home tending her terminally ill husband. I expect to see her with us again when she's released from this family service. I consider her one of the 36; she is not seen but she sustains our spirit.

I think also of the woman who on a rainy Seattle Saturday takes the bus downtown, transfers to Bellevue, then goes to a temple session before taking the cumbersome bus trip home again.

I think of the saint whose face glows in the temple. In a magnified form this glow is described as the fire of God. Personally I have seen this countenance of a bride — the face of my bride many years ago, and recently the face of my niece as a young bride. Rather than multiply examples, I would just note that the 36 is in each of us. Each of us can look for the image of Christ in every face.

May you build your foundation on a rock, the rock of Christ.

Our Divinity

Mormons view humans as offspring of God with the potential to become like God.

20 Wrought upon and cleansed
Ward Conference – 2/15/98

Our stake theme this year is taken from Moroni, chapter 6, which concludes with instruction to conduct meetings after the manner of the workings of the Spirit. In light of this, I question my own faith in putting words on paper before appearing at this pulpit. My justification, and I may have to repent of this some day, is that I am yet intimidated by having to stand here, and find myself not as singularly attentive to the Spirit here as in my solitary chamber. My assigned time is ten minutes. I would have you nourished by the good word of God, and I assure you that you would leave this meeting hungry if you had to pick through my spontaneous rambling.

Our theme "nourished by the good word of God" carries two implicit charges within a given context of action. One, to comprehend what *is* the "good word of God." The object of our aspiration remains an unknown until we learn that. What is the "good word"? The word is "in the beginning… it was with God and it is God." When we apply the Word as sacred writing, as our standard to measure the world and ourselves, then we make ourselves open to the Word.

Two, to feed upon the Word, to let ourselves be nourished by the Word. Nourish is to take in for the purpose of building up, of maturing. Ezekiel is told: "eat this scroll... So I opened my mouth, and He gave me this scroll to eat, as He said to me, 'Mortal, feed your stomach and fill your belly with this scroll' (Ezekial 3:1-3, The Jerusalem Bible translation)." In modern psychological terms, it is to incorporate, to take into our character, and into our lives. Not just put on, like a Sunday-go-to-meeting-suit, but to take in, to let it become part of our being.

Prepare for a feast. Open yourself to the Word. Start with chapter 6 of Moroni. Scan verses 1 through 4 for the pre-conditions, for what are presented as givens when we take up our theme: 1. live a life worthy of baptism, 2. come forth with a broken heart and a contrite spirit, 3. bear witness that your repentance is real, and 4. be determined to serve Christ to the end.

Now reflect upon verse 4: "And after they had been received unto baptism, and were wrought upon and cleansed... ."

Wrought: formed, shaped, made by hand, as in wrought iron, the passive form of the old English wright, to construct with one's hand, to make, to act on a material.

We mortals delight in taking action, witness the pure delight of the toddler in standing upright and moving its body through space — basically the same delight, I suspect, as scientists hurdling rockets out into space. But to be acted upon, to be wrought upon, that is a different matter. To experience this let us go with Jeremiah to the potter's house (Chap. 18).

A lump of clay is a lowly thing, and we mortals are lumps of clay. The master scoops us from the slime in which we lie and plops us upon his wheel. We are rotated through the days of our life, spun until our heads are dizzy, until we no longer know left from right, up from down, until we question our own sense of direction, our own notion of good and evil. Then, and first then, does the Master wright us. He puts his thumb into the middle of the mess that we are and applies just enough pressure, and this while holding us intact with the palm of His hand. This action, applied with firmness and consistency, molds us, opens us up, pushes us up toward heaven, makes us upright.

A lump of mortal clay is a lowly thing, but a vessel of the Lord is divine form, and we rightfully say, "God be praised."

Raw clay is a fragile thing, and we mortals are fragile. We are bent and deformed by the waters of time; we cannot resist deformity, decomposition, and corruption. We are subject to the pressures of the moment, the fad of the day, the tide of popular opinion. Green stock must be fired. We must go through the raging furnace that extracts our impurities and leaves us impervious to time and cleanses our soul. We must be subjected to the blazing tongues of wanton gossip, to the fiery heat of adversity, to the scorching devastation of illness and pain. We must go through the fiery furnace, be tried and tested by the fires of the Spirit.

Raw clay is a fragile thing, but a fired crucible, tried and tested by the Spirit, is a steadfast rock, and we rightfully say, "God be praised."

A hardened mud pot is a plain thing, and we mortals are plain in the glory of the Lord. The Wright smears us with foreign elements, the pigments and hues that span the full spectrum of His light. We are exposed to situations, ideas, and dilemmas to which we say, "When did I sign up for this?" Then back into the furnace, so the coloring becomes one with us. This time and again, one color after another, one situation following another. This, until we too are on the cross of our lives, when we feel hung up to dry, when nothing comes from our mouth except, "My God, my God, why hast thou forsaken me." (Matt. 27:46) We have been wrought upon, and cleansed by the power of the Holy Ghost. Then we are numbered among the people of Christ. Then we desire to be remembered, and nourished by the good word, and kept in the right way.

It is a terrifying thing to take on all that crosses our way, but a child of God is sustained by eternal benevolence. We have endured many things, and shown ourselves willing to endure all things, and we rightfully say, "Father, into thy hands I commend my spirit."

Wouldn't it be nice, nice and easy, to extend the Word to others without having to be shaped, fired, and tried ourselves? But then all that we would have to offer our fellow mortals is a soggy lump of clay, without shape, durability, or color. The Doctrine & Covenants is emphatic: "Seek not to declare my word, but first seek to obtain my word...hold your peace; study my word... until you have obtained all... ." (D&C 11:21)

What allows the clay to go through the process which molds it to what it has always been in the eyes of the Master? For one thing, it helps to not know what life has in store for you. The full vision would be overwhelming. Can we rely upon our smarts, our cleverness, our strength, our stamina? Not in this, not in the critical task of mortality. In this we can rely only upon Him who knows us from the beginning, before we were in the womb, upon Him who writes the story of our existence from the beginning, and puts the finishing touches on the life which we walk in faith. He awaits us upon fulfillment of this life; He awaits within us for our completion. Until then, let us know one another by name, let us feast together on the good word of God, let us keep one another in the right way. Let us stay awake in the Lord, above all, let us rely for our help solely upon our Redeemer, our Savior, our Lord, Jesus Christ. Amen.

21 Understanding our relationship to scripture
Sacrament Meeting – 3/22/98

I would share some thoughts about the difference between talking and living. Talking about the gospel is not the same as living the gospel. Talking about the word of wisdom is not the same as living the word of wisdom. We can talk about the benefits of clean living while poisoning our body, and we can live in a righteous and healthy manner without much reflection. Talking *may* promote a manner of living, or it may be a substitute for living. I am rather removed from the current dating scene, but I recall that when on the third date your date says, "Let's talk about our relationship," you know that the relationship is over. Good things often proceed on their own without a lot of talk.

There is a place for examination of relationships, but it is an unsatisfying substitute for the relationship itself. I enjoy cookbooks with pictures of lavish dishes when I have a full stomach. But pictures are no substitute for food for the stomach. I would have you feed on the gospel and not just talk about it.

The philosopher-psychiatrist Karl Jasper makes a useful distinction between two approaches to comprehension. He notes the difference between *erklären* and *verstehen*. The former is to clarify, to view from a perspective. The latter is to understand. *Verstehen* is to have appreciation of where one stands. Both have their place. When I go to see my doctor, accountant or mechanic, I want some perspective on my problem. I want something more than an empathic understanding that my situation is a mess. I already know that. I want an objective view in order to begin to untangle the problem. The same holds for scholars. Their perspective can be useful to clarify matters, but it is a distant perspective, a holding oneself away from the subject matter.

In all that we do we take a stance. We position ourselves as observing from a distance or as taking in. This applies, for example, in our study of the Old Testament prophets. We can look at the Jacob-Esau story as something to examine from a historical perspective, or we can take it into our lives. We can see Jacob and Esau as two aspects of our own nature. We read that Jacob and Esau were already fighting in the womb. That is a tip-off that we are dealing with something other than obstetrical practices of the ancient Hebrews. So when Isaac gives his blessing, he observes that the hand is the hand of Esau but the voice is the voice of Jacob. Esau is the action — something not to be deprecated. The voice, the desire, comes from within; this is Jacob, Jacob who receives the blessing. We are blessed for the desire of our heart, whether or not we can effect action in the world. We are blessed for what is in our heart.

When we live the scriptures rather than subject them to critical scrutiny, we do not speak of deceit. We understand that God extends his grace for what we want to do as well as for what we are able to do. May we find a fullness in the scriptures, live them, and receive the blessings of the Lord for it. This I say in the name of Jesus Christ. Amen.

Eternal Striving

This theme is an obvious favorite of Bishop Clark. In expounding it, he draws upon Hebrew biblical texts, homilies from his observations of nature, his existential leanings and examples drawn from down-to-earth living.

22   On sacrifice
Sacrament Meeting – 8/4/98

President Tucker recently advised bishops that they not only may instruct from the pulpit, but that they should do so regularly. The best instruction I can imagine your getting from me would be my standing here and requesting some members of the congregation to come forward and to share the working of the Lord in their lives. Sister A., please come to the pulpit and tell us of your physical pain and emotional travail in caring for three generations of loved ones. Brother B., please recount how you kept trying to provide for your family and to serve others notwithstanding all your own self-loathing. Sister C., please read off the list of doubts and inconsistencies you've struggled with over the years while trying to maintain membership in the community of believers. Brother D., please share the agony of living with the gossip and personal attacks on your character and style of interacting when you tried to fulfill your callings as best you could.

In short, I would have many of you tell of your sacrifice. Your own personal, intense, problematic, barely explainable sacrifice. But I hesitate to even use the word. Sacrifice, you might have noticed, has gotten a bad press. The word "sacrifice" has been hijacked. It has effectively lost its value as a carrier of a concept that can be used in meaningful discourse. It has become demonized, somewhat like "the religious right" in some political circles, or "liberal" in others. Sacrifice evokes images of some savage Aztec ripping out a bleeding heart, or a Hebrew nomad slaughtering some animal. It is used on kids to ask them to give up something that is dear to them. We adults may fool ourselves, but the kids are not fooled. I have verified this in the nursery. When I am two years old and big enough to stand on my own feet, walk across the room and pick out my toy, I am not about to share it with some smaller kid because some big person tells me to learn to sacrifice. When I share under these conditions, it is because the big person is so much bigger, and because they hand out the snacks and I just might not get mine if I do not fork over the loot.

To circumvent the deeply ingrained negative connotations of an important concept, I would introduce a new word. Actually, I would revive an ancient, God-given word: *qorbon*. Try it out for yourself. *Qorbon*. Has a nice ring. Anyone yet feel offended? Guilty? Overwhelmed? Good! Let us go on.

The verb *qarab* is variably translated as "come near, come nigh, approach, or draw near." First in Leviticus is *qarab* translated as "offer," as in "offer of the sacrifice, of the young bullock, the goat, or the burnt offering." *Qarab* is to approach or to come near to. To sacrifice to God is to approach God, to draw near to God. Whatever we may bring with us into a relationship, be it a bullock or goat, a burnt offering, a contrite heart, or (in the case of a young newly-wed couple) a declaration of unlimited love, the critical aspect is our approaching the object of our worship.

A *qorbon* to God requires the person offering it to draw near to God. We cannot send our *qorbon* by UPS or parcel post. We cannot hire someone to pick it out for us, wrap it up pretty, and drop it off at the doorstep, like a floral bouquet or a singing telegram. By its very definition, a *qorbon* requires the person offering it to approach the object of her or his affection. By definition, the biblical definition of the word, you do not bring a sacrifice unless you bring it, unless you approach the object of your attention.

William Phelps had it right when he penned: "Sacrifice brings forth the blessings of heaven." The sacrifice of "Brother Joseph" lay not in his giving up his life, but in his taking on the attributes of the Lord. "Praise to the man who communed with Jehovah."

Sacrifice brings forth blessings not because of what we give up, but because of what we take on. A sacrifice is not divesting ourselves of a good or service for whatever purpose and from whatever motivation. A sacrifice is assuming a closer relationship. A sacrifice to God is to approach God, to take on His qualities, to be closer to Him. A sacrifice for a spouse, friend, or parent is an effort to come closer to them, to appreciate their qualities, to get to know them better.

To sacrifice for your spouse, your family, or your dear friends means that you approach them. You draw near to them. You open yourself up to them, confide in them, and take in and treasure their confidences. You become less distant and more intimate. You change where you are in relation to them, and in the process you change who you are. This is the essence of sacrifice.

To give up some time or money in order to ease the life of someone else in your family or in this congregation may be an admirable thing, but by itself it is not a sacrifice in the biblical sense of the word. You bring a *qorbon*, a biblical sacrifice, only if you bring yourself into the relationship. When you feel more caring and more loving, then you sacrifice. You sacrifice even if you bring more fire, discontent, and complaints into the relationship, if you change, if you move your position in life to be more closely bonded to them. You do not have to be happy to sacrifice, but you do have to be you, and you have to change who you are, where you stand in life, your position vis-a-vis the object of your sacrifice.

I would hope that henceforth in whatever context you hear the word "sacrifice," you can do a mental translation and say quietly to yourself "draw near to." To sacrifice all is to draw near with all that we have and all that we are. Can we imagine approaching God with anything less than every fiber of our body and every sentiment of our soul? If asked to "sacrifice" to serve as a visiting or home teacher, should we not want to draw near to our fellow saints, determine where they are at, and be closer to them? Can we not consider our sacrifice for our family to be our wish that they draw close to God, and so we bring forth godly behavior to promote this.

Draw near to God! Be closer to those whom you want to love. Live in the confidence that God awaits with aching heart your approach to Him, so He can shower his blessings upon you. Live in the quiet contentment that your drawing near to those whom you love here is doing nothing less than what God does for all of us.

This I pray to Him who offered His Only Begotten for our behalf, in the name of the Only Begotten who sacrificed all for us. Amen.

23 The sound of *shin*
Sacrament Meeting – 4/10/99

As an undergraduate studying the history of science, my mentor thought it desirable to have me attend the monthly graduate student research-in-progress seminars. The topics were exoteric and the content matter way above my level of comprehension. The presenters were speaking English, but I did not understand half the words they were using. You might already know how graduate students hone in and get their theses completed. As Richard Bushman, who wrote a biography of Joseph Smith, once explained it: "You take a small nail, sharpen it, and pound it to death." Freed from having to concern myself about the content, I could listen to the process, focus on the argumentative style, and reflect upon the rhetoric.

In that spirit, I would now offer a reflection upon the language of the Bible, Hebrew — the language God gave for the Holy Word, and preserved through the millennia up to the present day. Hebrew is different from other languages in that in its very structure is embedded the Way of Life (or the Plan of Salvation, as Mormons would say). For example, the very first letter refers to an emergence from another sphere or world — a pre-mortal life, if you will.

Each letter is part of a numerical sequence. Each has a name and pronunciation, and each has a particular meaning. The letter that heralds the appearance of the created world, the first letter in the Bible, is pronounced "b" — an explosive, forceful sound, signaling in its very sound something akin to the "Big Bang" theory of modern science. The name of this letter, *beth*, means house and is preserved in this usage, for example in *beth-lethem*, Bethlehem, the House of Bread. *Beth* is the house of this world, the abode of our mortal existence, the created universe in which we live.

Today I would make a couple of observations about the next-to-last letter, *shin*. *Shin* has the meaning "tooth." What is the significance of a "tooth"? The tooth is the instrument in the front of the mouth that tears food into pieces. It shreds what we ingest into digestible portions. It separates and divides; it differentiates and distinguishes. When we hear a piece of uncertain news, we do not just swallow it whole. We say, "I'll chew on that a bit"

Differentiation can lead to differential treatment and segregation of particular parts. We chew on a prune, swallow the pulp, and spit out the pit. We don't swallow things we do not want to take in, because after swallowing, the rest of the digestive process is automatic — unconscious, if you will. We do not make a conscious decision which molecules will be absorbed through the lining of the gut and become part of our very physical structure and which will pass through unabsorbed. This is why we are careful what we expose ourselves too. Once taken in, we have minimal conscious control over which images and experiences will become part of our character.

Differentiation and segregation are conflicted values in late 20th-century America. They can promote diversity; they may also allow different and unfair treatment. Even given the best of intentions, differentiation brings on suffering. Just reflect back on your adolescence when you were separating from your parents. A painful time. And equally hard on the parents. It is hard to see your children make their own decisions when you are aware of the superficiality of their reasons and the inadequacy of their reflections on the potential consequences of their actions. And as parents, you are usually right. My father, upon retiring from ranching, had to leave the community, had to go on a mission in a distant state, to get away from surveying the work of the hands less competent and caring than his.

The tooth tears asunder, and suffering inevitably results. Suffering is a fact of life; the question is: what do we make of it? What do we have to say about the suffering intrinsic to separateness? How does this play out in our life? How does this come out of our mouth?

Here the pronunciation of *shin* has something to tell us. The letter has two pronunciations. One is *sin*, a sharp hissing sound, like Satan, like serpent, like the Hebrew word for the opposite of right. The other is a broad "sh." The difference in these two sounds lies in where the emphasis is put. The letter can be thought of as a form drawn by the hand of God — starting from the center of His presence and extending outward to the outmost reach of man. If the emphasis is put on its origin, on its close affinity to God, then the broad "sh" sound is generated. If the emphasis is on man's concern, then the hissing "s" of Satan is heard.

This understanding sheds light upon a passage in Judges, chapter 12 in which it is reported that the Gileadites slew 42,000 Ephraimites. "And the Gileadites took the passages of Jordan before the Ephraimites; and it was so, that when those Ephraimites which were escaped said, Let me go over; that the men of Gilead said unto him, Art thou an Ephraimite? If he said, Nay; then said they unto him, Say now Shibboleth: and he said Sibboleth; for he could not frame to pronounce it right. Then they took him, and slew him at the passages of Jordan: and there fell at that time of the Ephraimites forty and two thousand."

Here the Ephraimites were differentiated; they were not close to their origin. They did not have "sh" in their mouth; they were far from God. It is reported that they were slain, but in essence they were already dead to the power that enlivens us all each day. They spoke of their own interests ,and it manifested itself in what they said. It is not, as the so-called higher critics of the Bible might maintain, that the Gileadites slew the Ephraimites because they had a collective speech impediment.

When we are far from God, it shows in our utterances, in our behavior, in how we live out our lives. We live here as separate human beings, and we suffer in our isolated, separate worlds. But we can yet yearn to be close to God — and our yearning will be reflected in our speech.

My final reference comes from the hymnal, number 232. "Let us oft speak kind words to each other; At home or where'er we may be; Like the warblings of birds on the heather; The tones will be welcome and free. They'll gladden the heart that's repining; Give courage and hope from above; And where the dark clouds hide the shining; Let in the bright sunlight of love. Oh, the kind words we give shall in memory live; And the sunshine forever impart. Let us oft speak kind words to each other; Kind words are sweet tones of the heart."

I pray this in the name of Jesus Christ, Amen.

24 The short cut; do you really think there is one?
Sacrament Meeting – 8/08/99

I invite the children to come to the front. You can sit on the floor in front of where I am speaking. I have something to show you.

Do you see what I have in my hand? It's an egg. Now be very quiet and listen very closely. Can you hear that peck, peck, peck coming from the inside? What is making that noise? – A tiny chick! Very good guess. Now why would the chick be pecking away at the shell of this egg? Because it wants to get out! Another very good guess. Think how hard that little chick is going to have to work to break through this shell. That's a lot of work for a very little chick. What if we helped the chick to get out by breaking the shell? Seems like a good idea? The chick wouldn't have to work so hard? Whoops, another hand from the back. Not good, you say. Why not? Because it's not ready to come out yet. When it's ready to come out it can get out on its own! Sounds good! Another eager hand! Because if it comes out before it's ready it won't be ready to live. Sounds good again. What a smart Primary we have!

You can help me with another problem. Have you seen the little birdies when they get out of the nest and are about ready to fly? Do you notice how they sit on a branch next to the nest and flap their wings while they hop along the branch? And then they flap their wings when they hop from one branch to the next. And then they flap their wings and hop-fly from one branch to the next. Such a lot of effort! What if we just climbed up the tree and tossed them in the air? Not a good idea? Because they're not ready to fly? And think of the cat waiting on the ground. Definitely not a good idea!

Now why do you suppose it is that your parents are so slow to let you walk across the street by yourself? Or go to the store alone? Yeah, you've got it.

You can go back to your seats and sit with your parents. While you do that I shall spell it out for your parents. They are no longer as fast on their feet as you are. Chicks and children need to get out on their own. But it needs to be at the right time, and it needs to be with due effort. The idea of a shortcut may seem a way to save time and avoid pain – but most shortcuts do not really work.

Now an object lesson for those of us closer to the other end of life. Why can't we just hasten the death process when it is clear that we shall shortly emerge from this shell of a world and break forth into the next? Same principle. We need to be strengthened for the tasks we will face there. And what are these tasks? We have, I suspect, about as much an idea as the newborn babe knows of its mortal life tasks when it emerges from the womb. It is right to do what we can to preserve our health, to avoid unnecessary suffering and pain, to promote our physical and emotional well-being. It is wrong to presume we can take life in our own hands. Life is God's gift to us. Suicide, and its extension, our thinking any person can decide how long another human being should live, is grasping for what is in God's hands — life itself.

You would have thought we would have learned such simple lessons, but the temptation to take the short-cut seems to be increasing. This mind-set of a quick fix, I believe, contributes toward the more notorious social evils of our time. We want to feel good and to avoid pain. My sources on the street inform me the best way is feel good immediately without relying upon anyone else is an injection of quality heroin in a convenient vein. Similarly, gambling seems a shortcut to immediate riches. If you pick the right number, you win the lotto. My in-house sage characterizes the lotto as the state tax on stupidity. Its evil lies not only in taking money from the poor, but in its corruption of the values of honest work and sustained effort. The same applies to the stock speculation manifest in Seattle in the late 1990's. If you picked the right stock, you could retire within five years. The illusionary promise is likewise implicit in pornography: immediate, effortless gratification without the anguish of courtship. "Does she love me? Does she not?" And without the agony of vulnerability. "If I proclaim my interest and desire, will I be rejected and scorned?"

The short-cut mentality is not just "of the world;" it inveigles itself into our daily life and practices. Listen to us: "Did we say the prayer on the food?" Once said and done, our prayer can be checked off and forgotten until the next sit-down. Why do we not say to ourselves with each bite: "Am I blessing God for this morsel of food I now put into my mouth?" Is our relationship to God one of the past perfect tense, "I have done," or the present progressive, "I am doing."

When the visiting teaching supervisor calls on September 2 and asks if you have done your visiting teaching for August, you may answer, "Yes." Don't take up her precious time with existential quibbling about the nature and quality of your teaching. By definition, if August is past, then your visiting teaching for August is done. Now, if she phones on August 29 and asks, you must, if you are a truthful good and faithful servant, answer, "No," because you are still assigned those sisters, and two days remain in which the need for blessings and help may be evident to you, so you are not "done" with your visiting teaching.

When a member is sick, either in body or spirit, why is our question: "Have the Elders given her a blessing?" Why not the question: "Are we, her friends and neighbors, actively involved in blessing her life: in a phone call, in a short note, in a visit with a pound cake or a flower, in a passing thought, in a silent prayer, in an offer to watch the kids for an evening."

The human tendency to convert the means to the end into an end in itself can detract us from our ultimate goal. A temple marriage is a covenant made before God in His Holy House. I cannot image a better beginning to a life together. But when this beginning is considered an end in itself, as if a temple marriage were the guarantee of marital bliss, then comes disappointment, with the inevitable need to work through human differences, and perhaps even a sense of betrayal that the temple marriage didn't "deliver" what it promised. It is we who make the promise to work at marriage so that our effort may bring down the blessings of heaven.

Likewise, to have a friend is a wonderful thing. But friendships don't come ready-made off-the-rack. Friendships are made, made by making oneself vulnerable, by reaching out, laborious effort, correcting misunderstandings and maturing beyond supposed slights and real injuries. Just to ask, "Do I have a friend?" risks a disappointing answer and continued loneliness. To ask, "Am I working to make a friend?" brings friendship and joy in the process.

We may resolve to identify and avoid illusionary shortcuts in our life. We may decide to offer the prayer of the proverbial Christian who say, "Lord, I want patience, and I want it right now!" But do not imagine that the Christian virtues of patience, long-suffering, and enduring to the end are merely slowness, low expectations, and inertia. We have all gone through the pains of birth, and we all will surely go through the pangs of death-birth, but we don't have to be Pollyannaish about it. In the Liberty jail, Joseph Smith voiced his complaints. He was not told that he was stupid and to shut up, nor that he should cease whining and be grateful for what he did have, nor that he lacked faith and vision. No, he was told: "Thine adversity and thine afflictions shall be but a small moment." A small moment, but a moment of feeling abandoned and resentful. Such also belongs at times to life.

Time is the stuff of life. Time is a gift, a divine gift. Time is governed by the Lord. We are given time to discover who we are by having opportunity to play out the becoming of our being, to discover who we are inside eternally. We may well be a faithful daughter or son, a good friend, a devoted spouse, a providing and guiding parent. We come to know this as we experience it, and experience requires time. Experience involves mistakes, missteps, miscalculations. We partake of the tree of good and evil. And from the totality of our experience, sanctified by the grace and mercy of our Savior, we are ultimately released from the confines of time and may again partake of the tree of life that is momentarily forbidden us.

May we use our time well. This is the day of our repentance, and for us this day is continually renewed until the day we die, the moment we pass to a more sublime sphere. Do not think that you need to be perfect now. Know that you are loved now and share your love. Let us build up one another, and build up the kingdom. No short-cuts. Back to pecking on that shell.

25   A question without an answer
Fast and Testimony Meeting – 1/02/00

I recently came across an old saying: "The question without an answer is hell". If you trace the words back to their origins, you will see that question and hell do have the same root. But the parent of any four-year-old doesn't need a dictionary to know how repetitive questions can be anything but heaven.

"Why do I have to go to bed? Why is it time? Why is it the end of the day? Why did the sun set? Why does the earth go around the sun? Why did God make it that way? ..."

Life is the question. Life, and all aspects of it, is one continual question. Our response is the answer, and the question goes on as long as life does.

In regard to your church calling, the question is: "How do I fulfill my calling? What really is my calling? What am I directly called to do in life without an explicit assignment from someone else?"

Or in regard to something more enduring and central to our lives: "Why do I have no prospects of ever having children? Or, why do I have the children that I have? Or, why has my experience with my children been such that I look back at it with such moments of pain and regret?"

When your life is a question without an answer, I do have a couple of suggestions. One is to change the question. It is a common human tendency when we see life is going badly (as we see it) to ask, "Why is God punishing me?" I've found that question to be not very useful. The most obvious answers are that either God is mean, or that I deserve to be punished because I am guilty. I can not accept the notion that God is mean, and I have found that feeling guilty without a good reason does not get us very far. A more useful question is: "What am I to learn from this situation?"

Take, for example, what are we to learn when our joints increasingly creak? Maybe to slow down and to try not to do so much. Maybe to give up our pretense of independence and to accept our infirmities and the need for help from others. Maybe we are being told, "My child, I am making this world a bit less comfortable so that you will be a bit more ready to come home to me."

If we are in a given life situation, what are we to learn? Sometimes it seems we are stuck with a job until we learn to get it right. And sometimes I think what we have to learn is to quit trying to get it right.

My second suggestion is to change the emphasis of the question. Instead of asking, "Why does God *pick* on me?", try shifting the emphasis to: "Why does God pick on *me*?" Each of us is, after all, the center of the universe, at least, the center of *our* universe. So ask: "Why is God, in all His magnificence and glory, paying particular attention to me?" The answer is usually that He is trying to get your attention. He is trying to get you to be mindful of Him. When we are in good health and fair spirits, thinking we are on top of the world, we tend to forget about Him. It is when we see our world going badly and we feel bad that we tend to turn to Him.

He wants us to turn to Him. He wants us to be close to Him. He loves us, and rejoices when we return His love and show this love in our love for one another. May we do so, I pray in the name of Jesus Christ.

26 Let us labor diligently
Ward Conference – 1/21/01

I have three items to address this afternoon: first, an accounting of the ward activity in the past year; second, a public expression of gratitude for all who have served us so well; and third, a commentary upon the stake theme for this coming year.

First, I have here a 45-page ward history for the past year — compiled by our ward historian, Donna Baird. No, I'm not about to read it from the pulpit. We are putting copies into the hands of the Priesthood and the auxiliary leaders to lend out for your perusal, and we present a copy of it to the stake presidency.

Second, I want to thank publicly those sisters and brothers sustained who provide such dedicated service. Thanks also to all who act upon their personal revelation to help the widows and orphans among us. There is no formal church calling to pick up Cheerio crumbs after meetings, to wipe off more of the lavatory basin than you personally soiled, to hold the fussy child of an overly burdened mother sitting next to you, to pray for and with those who falter, to contribute time and money in a private capacity, to be of service in the secular community, and to live as a beacon of virtue and truth. I consider these unassigned services to be pure religion. My profound and enduring thanks to you who perform these secular sacraments.

Third, my commentary today addresses the stake scriptural theme for the year. Turn to Moroni 9:6. The abbreviated version reads: "…let us labor diligently… for we have a labor to perform … that we may conquer the enemy of all righteousness, and rest our souls in the kingdom of God."

Remarkable is not the exhortation to labor diligently; *that* we can find in dozens of other scriptural passages, in the urging of our parents, and in the secular world, for example, in pushing to meet new sales goals. Remarkable is the context. This is the second recorded epistle to Moroni from his father near the end of Mormon's leadership of the Nephite people — militarily remarkable and spiritually futile. Mormon records the contemporary condition in this the next-to-last chapter of his transmitted writings.

Scripture becomes meaningful, I believe, when we let it voice our inner selves, when we read it as our inner convictions and hidden aspirations, as an account of all that we would do with our miserable lives except for the weakness of our flesh and our limited circumstances.

Mormon has been fighting a losing cause. His own valiant resolutions and diligence have been futile in the face of his people's depravity. Think of when you have been fighting a losing cause. Read this not as an historical document of long ago and far away. Let it give voice to your life at this hour and place. Yours is the resolve and diligence, and yours is the slide into depravity. Are there not times, even now, when your resolve and efforts are pulled under by the momentum of your people, of your bodily appetites and weaknesses, of your frittering away the late hours when you should be sleeping, of your rolling over in bed when you should be arising, of your stuffing your mouth with an extra cookie when you have resolved to use time diligently and to curb your appetite. This, for you, is a commentary upon your people, upon your material life — when your inner Mormon would have led you to a righteous victory.

Read this scripture for its personal application to your life as if it were voiced on this 21st day of January. I shall

Eternal Striving

voice one rendition. As you follow along, translate it into you own current life situation.

Moroni, chapter 9, verse 1: To my dearest son, to the visible manifestation of my will and of my highest desires in the temporal sphere, to my tangible hope for the future. I write once more so that you may know I yet live; my noble desires and aspirations for our legacy are yet alive. But what I have to say is heavy.

Verse 2: I look at my life course and see my ongoing struggle with my dark side. I have been in mortal combat, and frankly we have lost big time. Many of my principals have been killed and I have lost much of what has sustained me in past battles.

Verse 3: I fear for the very survival of my goodness in the mortal sphere; my body resists exhortations to repentance. (I really must resist that second cookie, but I battle myself.)

Verse 4: I keep trying, but as surely as I speak God's truth, my people, my body, rebels — and that with a vengeance. (Might as well have a third cookie because I've already blown my diet.)

Verse 5: My life course blinds itself to its natural end. I've lost my sense of bonding, and am stuck in my recrimination. (I'm so bad I'll woof down that fourth cookie.)

Verse 6: (and here comes our theme): At this moment, my own dear promise for the future, notwithstanding my frailty of flesh and weakness of resolve, let's get our act together and really try this time. If we do not try, we will surely lose. We have a work to do as long as this old body has breath. Our task: to strive against the source of our unrighteousness so that we can find rest in our own divinity. And when we acknowledge our own divinity (even in the moment of our deepest depravity), we can recognize the presence of God in all that surrounds us. Then we have conquered; then we are in our eternal rest.

Scripture has the quality of being a perfect mirror. In it we see a perfect reflection of who we are at the present moment. So my reading is not precisely your reading. And I hope that your reading when I stood up to speak is not your reading now.

What do I find remarkable about this chapter? When — to all appearances — the battle is lost, the war is hopeless and our world is about to be obliterated, the voice of the Father addresses us: "My beloved son, my dearly beloved daughter. I know how My world appears to you: squalor, pettiness, vengeance, indolence, undisciplined anger, recurrent strife [and this describes our side, these sentiments are within us]. But I will not leave you abandoned here even though the war appears hopeless. Do not be deceived by appearances. I am with you through all your trials."

Our task is to move on, to labor diligently. Our condemnation lies not in what we have or have not done with our lives to date. No, we are condemned "if we cease to labor." For we have a labor to perform. God knows what we should make of our lives. We find out only as we make it happen — and it is our destiny to make it happen while housed in the miserable body that cannot resist even a second cookie. Don't dwell upon a recitation of your failings! Your past is already written. Our life from this moment on is spread out in front of us. In this present moment we are to find our eternal self. This self finds its rest only in what can aptly be described as a kingdom, the kingdom of God. In this kingdom we reside with God, with the spirit of God infusing every fiber of our being in every passing moment. We may live in this kingdom in this very moment, and in every moment of our mortal passage.

May we be open to this realization of God's ever-presence in our life, even now, while in this tabernacle of clay. This I pray in the name of Jesus Christ, through whom this reality is actualized in our mortal lives. Amen.

27 Quiet and assurance forever
Ward Conference – 1/21/02

I learned a thing or two during my stint in the military. For example, when attending an official function with the top brass, you put on your dress uniform. So, I have my dark blue suit and black toed shoes.

Another year, another ward conference, another bishop's report — with a three-part assignment: render an accounting of our stewardship, introduce the 2002 stake theme, and give my personal testimony and benediction — all this without infringing upon the time allotted for PresidentTucker.

The written annual history of the ward, so ably and lovingly compiled once again by our ward historian, Donna Baird, puts into print the more observable ward activities. This is available for your perusal through your priesthood and auxiliary leaders. Not committed to paper (but, I trust, noted by the recording angels) are the many, many examples of ward members showing faith and perseverance in the face of all kinds of adversities: financial woes, individual temptations, personal weaknesses, and our worries about health, well-being, financial security, personal safety, and eternal salvation.

For the 2002 stake theme, turn to Isaiah 32:17. "And the work of righteousness shall be peace; and the effect of righteousness quietness and assurance for ever," or in an alternate translation: "and the effect of righteousness, calm and confidence forever."

Perpetual calm and confidence: from whence comes this? Not from our own scheming and striving. Isaiah portrays what comes of our trying to appropriate and run God's creation in verses 13 and 14: a world overgrown with briers and thistles, abandoned palatial dwellings, a perpetually barren desert, a joy only to wild asses. What a fitting metaphorical description of the scene at 4th and Olive in downtown Seattle on Saturday night at 12 midnight — and of the drug district of our soul in the midnight of our despair.

From this scene of wanton depravity and hopeless barrenness comes the promise of perpetual calm and confidence. Not through our efforts, but when (verse 15) "the spirit be poured upon us from on high." Then the wilderness becomes fruitful, and the produce of the field becomes a veritable forest of growth — without our tending it. Abundance beyond measure, as a gift from God. All who sow (verse 20) are blessed, for the fruit is so abundant that cattle can roam freely through the vegetable garden. No need to fence out the livestock; our animal nature can feed to abundance on the tastiest produce because we now live from the outpouring of the bounty of the Lord.

Isaiah, like all scripture, has an eternal source and an everlasting application. This blessing is ours now. It is a gift from on high that is poured down upon us.

I reflect that it is a common tendency in the first half of life to focus upon getting things from the world: toys at Christmas, presents on birthdays, education for employment, a down-payment on a house, investment in children — which is beyond any monetary value. But in the second half of life, the challenge is not conquering the outside world, but in yielding our inner world to the wondrous fate that God has provided for us, a fate which we can hope for and have faith in, but cannot see nor even faintly imagine in its glory and eternal potential, in a word, yielding to God and His eternal plan for us.

In conclusion, my personal testimony and benediction. From my youth on I have been slow of speech, often tongue-tied to the point of incoherence, and have been hesitant to speak of more than I can deliver. Hence you have rarely heard me expressing that the Church is true, that the gospel has been restored, that my wife loves me more than I deserve. If my actions do not bespeak my convictions, then my convictions are a sham and are better not voiced. God will judge my soul, and I believe passionately in His wisdom and grace. I have utter confidence He will accord me, and all of us, more compassion, understanding, clemency, graciousness, kindness, more divine love, than I could ever possibly imagine on this side of the veil.

God does pour out His blessings, and the most wondrous and lasting ones are the best disguised. I would that among the briers and thistles of your life you live in the perpetual calm and confidence, the eternal quietness and assurance, which comes from your awareness that the Spirit is poured down upon us from on high. Amen.

The Annual Cycle

Christmas

Mormons commemorate Christmas in their weekly sacrament meeting and customarily have no special service. When Christmas Day falls on Sunday, the standard practice is to hold Sacrament Meeting and forego other meetings.

28 Jesus comes
Christmas Program - 12/12/93

Today our Sacrament Meeting program is focused on our celebration of the coming of Jesus, our Savior. Granted, we are two weeks early, but that's alright, for if the Savior was born in the spring then we are a full four months early.

My text today comes from the book given the subtitle "Another Testament of Jesus Christ." Please open to the Book of Third Nephi, written by the son of Helaman in the meridian of time. Scan the text with me.

Verse 12: "... the voice of the Lord came ..."

Verse 13: "Lift up your head and be of good cheer..."

Verse 14: "...I come unto my own, to fulfill all things..."

(This is the text of the Christmas card greeting prepared by the bishopric for ward members this year. It was entrusted to your home teacher to deliver to you. I trust they have done so; if not, feel free to contact them and ask for a visit this month.)

My interest here is not in this message of good cheer, but rather in the preconditions to the voice of the Lord bringing this message. Turn back to verse 10 to read Nephi's experience before the voice of the Lord came.

Verse 10: "...Nephi... saw this wickedness of his people, his heart was exceedingly sorrowful."

Verse 11: "...he went out and bowed himself down upon the earth, and cried mightily to his God in behalf of his people, yea, those who were about to be destroyed... ."

Verse 12: "...he cried mightily unto the Lord all that day; and behold, the voice of the Lord came unto him... ."

Reflect upon the account. He saw wickedness: he was not blind to the evil around him, nor did he turn his back upon those doing evil. And there is no equivocation or sophistry in the name of "value conflict resolution." Nephi saw wickedness.

He was sorrowful, not indignant, not self-righteous, not condemnatory. He did not ask if they had brought evil upon themselves, if they had been led astray, if they deserved punishment. He was sorrowful, indeed exceedingly sorrowful.

He went out, he left the scene. He did not jump into the fray, did not indulge in philosophical reflection nor enter into a contentious debate.

He lowered himself down upon the earth; he humbled himself to the ground, and from this position he addressed God.

He cried, mightily, not for himself, but on behalf of his people. He cried out for their sake, for the sake of sinners. And he did this "all that day" – with persistence, and with faith. THIS is how effective work is done!!!

With what result?: "and behold the voice of the Lord came unto him... ." The word is given.

Read on in the account on your own time. There follow lies and deceit, but yet, in verse 22, we read: "the more part of the people did believe...".

The coming of Jesus is not a one-time thing, not an historical event in a distant time in a far-away place. Jesus comes into our life when we invite him in. This coming is the birth of the babe who redeems us.

In this vein I have one final story. This is of my great uncle Amasi. Just before we married, Barbara and I visited him in Farmington, Utah. He was then 102 years old. Being unsure of his driving, he rode his bicycle to work at the bank. Because in his youth he appeared too sickly for a solid life as a livestock owner or farmer, his father established a bank for him. So at 102 he would ride off to his desk at the bank. Truth be told, he came late and left early, and the acting director had to review all of his decisions and tidy up his desk after he walked out the door. But he did go to work, and then after work each day he would push the wheelchair of his invalid wife down the street so she could get some fresh air. But that is not my story.

My story is from my youth in northern Bear Lake valley, to which great uncle Amasi would come each Labor Day weekend with my grandfather Edward, a couple of other brothers — and some younger men (in their 60's or so) to do the driving. Grandfather habitually slept overnight with my uncle Melvin; Amasi would sleep with us on the Saturday night before the Sunday testimony meeting at which Uncle Joseph would always tell the same story of how he was struck on the head by his father throwing a chain over the load of logs to secure them in his rush to have the distinction of having the first logs out of the canyon to build up the new settlement of Twin Creeks, now Georgetown. But I digress again.

The story was told me several years after the fact. One year Amasi was awakened in the middle of the night by the baby, my younger sibling, crying in our parents' adjoining bedroom. He was kept awake by the baby's persistent crying. Amasi reflected upon the situation and did what he was wont to do. He climbed out of his warm bed in the dark of the night, knelt on the wooden floor, and prayed that the child would be stilled so that the mother could get some rest.

This shapes my life even now, even here. When a baby fusses in church, I'm inclined to say a silent prayer on behalf of the parent. A baby crying is an announcement of a new soul on earth. Praise God for an infant with lusty lungs. Quiet can promote a kind of reverence, but so can joyful praises to the Lord. A baby gives praise for life and salvation as well as it is able.

Let the babe be born! Let us rejoice in His birth! Let the child grow in us and lead us. Let us grow in the conviction that we are the children of a loving father, a father who sends his son to fulfill all things — all things including our eternal salvation and joy, even here in this season. Jesus comes. We are fulfilled by Him. We may extend his love to all other creatures.

29 Mary's burden
Christmas Day Sacrament Meeting – 12/25/94

I have a story for you. It involves a teenage, unwed mother with a promise of marriage. Her son was born in a shelter for the homeless. Then she and her partner hit the road again — headed for a place renown for its corruption and godlessness! Eventually her son took up a trade, but he quit his job, drifted about the countryside rabble-rousing for a couple or three years. Then the authorities caught him and summarily executed him. They did cut some legal corners, but people in the know assured the populace that he was a menace to organized society and the present danger to society justified the quick administrative action.

This is a rendition of the well-known story, if taken only as historical fact and put in modern jargon. Today I shall not elaborate upon this story, but say something about its context, about what precedes it.

It is said that the fruit of the garden is set in the seeds that are planted. The fruit can be foretold if you know what you plant. If you know the name of the seed, you know what comes in time, given proper care and nurture.

Consider Mary, the mother of this child. In the Greek account her name is Mariam. This is nothing other than a transliteration of the Hebrew *miryam*. *Miryam* is a word that bespeaks the concept of bitterness, or rebelliousness — resentment and rebellion being a usual human response to being given the bitter in life.

From her name we would expect Mary's fate to be one of struggling with the bitter. And this was her life. Whatever your life has brought you, compare it to how you would feel if you went through what Mary experienced. Have your child born in a barn and die at a public execution.

Have your pre-schooler wander off at the mall, only to be found three days later. Have your 12-year-old tell you in effect to mind you own business because he's doing deals on a level you don't even begin to understand.

If this were your fate, how would you square it with a memory of the messenger of the Lord addressing you: "You are highly favored, the Lord is with you: blessed are you among women." I suspect you would likely alternate between reflecting upon this greeting as a cruel hoax, and thinking it some incredible, inscrutable patriarchal blessing which you would read regularly with hardly a clue how it might be fulfilled.

Mary, Miryam, the bitter in our life, poses the question, "How can we consider ourselves to be a beloved daughter of God and simultaneously live with the bitterness and disappointments of our miserable life?" When life seems to play out without any satisfactory answer, look to its source. Peer into the seed, into the nucleus of the story. Look at where Mary comes from. The mother of Mary, according to tradition, is Anna, in Hebrew, *Channah.* Channah is the feminine form of *chen*, translated as grace or favor.

There is an illuminating tradition about Channah and the creation of the world. When God contemplated creation of the world, it is said, God's advisors, the hosts of angels around Him, heard out his plans, deliberated thoughtfully, and told God that His plans for creation were not feasible, could not be carried out. Mankind would be put into a world with too much temptation and too little strength. Mankind would go his own evil way, destroy himself and take down the world with him. Mankind would be blinded by his own pride, overcome by his own hubris, and end in certain destruction, in hell.

At this moment, it is said, Channah steps forward, announces herself by name, *channah*, and offers her daughter

Miryam as ready to carry the bitterness of the world, to suffer the bitter of all that creation will bring for the sake of love.

When Channah speaks, God says, "You have said the word: 'grace'. I can proceed with creation." Grace announcing herself allows God's work of creation and redemption to proceed.

The story of Channah is a variation of the account of the pre-mortal Christ presenting himself as a sacrifice to the world. We Mormons have long known the story; this is its telling in another idiom.

Another expression of this thought is voiced by saying, "The child is carried in the womb." The word for womb, in Hebrew *rechem*, is simultaneously the word for mercy or forgiveness. To bear a child is to have mercy. Only through mercy is the pain of disappointment and bitterness bearable. And forgiveness is inevitably necessary because mankind inevitably sins.

It is a bitter thing to bear the Christ child. The bitter can be borne only when it is borne in the grace of God's love.

It is bitter to extend yourself to another only to be misunderstood and hurt. Grace gives the assurance of God's understanding when our fellow man does not.

It is bitter to intend to do good and have it taken for evil and meanness. Grace gives the quiet reassurance that our intentions count when our execution is faulted.

It is bitter to see others cheat on exams and be rewarded with better grades. Grace gives a reward of the heart when the body is cheated.

It is bitter to have to acknowledge one's own weakness and pettiness. Grace gives a lifting of the soul, even when we don't deserve a break — especially when we don't "deserve it!"

This grace makes creation possible, makes our lives bearable. Let us forgive one another so we are open to recognizing God's forgiveness. Let us open our hearts to the Christ child. Let us bear the bitterness that comes with bringing Christ into our life and into the world. Let us speak out in grace and forgiveness so God may proceed with His creation, with His work, which is to bring to pass our eternal life and salvation

30 Shepherds in the field
Christmas program – 12/24/95

What should one say after so much has been said? I would look more closely at one aspect of this story. With me, read Luke 2:8-9, & 20.

8. And there were in the same country shepherds abiding in the field, keeping watch over their flock by night.

9. And, lo, the angel of the Lord came upon them, and the glory of the Lord shone round about them: and they were sore afraid.

20. And the shepherds returned, glorifying and praising God for all the things that they had heard and seen, as it was told unto them.

Let us reflect upon this phrase by phrase.

And there were in the same country. It is not clear what country is referenced: Judaea? Bethlehem? This introduction is quaint; it has an almost mythical quality. It is like beginning a story with "Once upon a time," or "Long ago and far away."

But this is from the Bible, which I consider not a fairy tale but God's universal word to each of his children. For one message to have infinite real applications requires a particular rhetorical style. This style is evident from the first page of the Bible. As each day of creation evolves from God's word, the scripture records: "God said...". If I were writing this piece of scripture, I would begin: "In the place where your essential being commences to enfold..."– and you would quickly stop reading such abstract, obtuse, forgettable words. I can't see a way to improve upon "God said...".

So how to present the concept? There is nothing better than to tell a story. Reflect upon one English use of the word "story:" it is one layer in a multi-storied building. A "story" must have multiple layers of meaning, or it is not a story. The literary devise here is to use symbols with universal application.

I can relate to the image of "shepherds." In Idaho the shepherd's job is to keep the herd together, safe from coyotes and occasional marauding bears. The Bible is replete with images of shepherds. Abraham, Isaac and Jacob all had multitudes of animals. I would not argue with biblical readers who argue that these ancient patriarchs did earn their living raising animals, but I choose to consider the specific historical facts to be incidental and the symbolic conveyance to be universal. So I read universal meaning into Jacob and his sons coming to Pharaoh in Egypt as shepherds, Moses tending the flocks of Jethro as a shepherd, and Jesus giving instruction to "feed my sheep."

A shepherd has his flock; the purpose of his life is to preserve the unity of this flock. A "good shepherd" is not just a Basque immigrant in the scrub brush of high mountain plains, but one who cares for his congregation, for those sisters on her visiting teaching list, for her family. First and foremost we are responsible for ourselves. Beyond that, I consider responsibility tied to the extent of our influence. A flock is not just a bunch of sheep, cows or goats; our flock is the totality of our own life. The flock we tend is the totality of our ideas, dreams, encounters, readings, conversations, experiences. Our flock encompasses all sorts of momentary dispositions and feelings: stubborn, compliant, gentle, passionate, pliable, charming, exciting, inspirational–as well as feelings that are annoying, putrid, infuriating, petty. We tend these, feed them, protect them, keep them for their eventual purpose.

Why have a flock at all? What is its purpose? In Idaho it was to get that annual check that paid the electrical bill and college tuition. The worth of an animal could be calculated precisely: the going price per pound times the number of pounds on hoof. But what is the purpose of our thoughts, our dreams, our feelings? Stated more simply, what is the purpose of our life?

In the Bible animals exist primarily as a sacrifice. The biblical word for sacrifice means simply "to bring oneself to God." To sacrifice is to bring everything in our life closer to God, to give life meaning in relation to God. Various sins, transgressions, and troubles, as well as our thanks and joy, are all moments that let us come closer to God — and move us along to the inspiring moment when we have a glimmer of what it might mean to bring a perfect sacrifice.

So the shepherds keep their animals in order to offer a sacrifice, to bring all their experience to God. A shepherd must repeatedly sacrifice his existing point-of-view, his old way of understanding, his sense of self-reliance, his pretense of self-determination.

In this light, reflect upon the mature Jesus's saying, "Leave the ninety and nine and seek out the one." This is poor economics but it is good salvation. To get ahead in the world you build on your strengths, cover your weaknesses, get a competitive advantage, sell your losers. But Jesus says, "Seek out that which challenges you, live in gentleness, take courage, apply patience, long-suffering, tolerance, compassion."

"Abiding in the field": a graphic picture of how the good shepherd lives. Bivouacking reads one translation. Not asleep in bed, not reveling in the tavern, not sitting around the campfire complaining about the drop in lamb prices. They were on the job, just doing what was theirs to do.

"Keeping watch by night." Translators stumble over this phrase. Some write "keeping guard of the night," or "through the night." The Living Bible doesn't even try; it omits the phrase entirely. The Word says "in the watches of the night."

Reflect upon how this phrase is used in the Bible. Look at the writings of the prophets. In the night, the priests of the house of God stand on the wall. With every watch of the night, the cry goes forth: "Watchman, how far is the night?" And the watchman must then answer that it is yet night. The night is divided into three or four watches. It is the last watch of the night that announces the coming of the new day. This is the watch of the darkest hour — just before the first break of day. Is it not so also in our lives?

You can use God's word to make changes, To change the world, apply God's word to history. To change yourself, apply it to yourself. Why yourself first? Consider whom you will be most concerned about when you face the judgment bar, and apply the word to that person or institution. If you are like me, you'll ask, how dark is it within me? It can be dark even in broad daylight. And not just dark because I am in financial straits or the boss is always on my case, but in my finding life itself meaningless because of my chaotic and distorted view of life.

But for whomever walks in the way to God, seeking Him with longing, there comes the moment when he begins to see — starting with the outlines, which then grow ever brighter and clearer. Then the watchman, the shepherd, may announce the signs of day.

"And, lo." In current jargon: "Hey, you! Listen up, here comes what you've been waiting for."

"Angel" is a messenger. A message from God came upon them. We might say: "It came to them" — meaning they received inspiration, insight and clarification.

Consider this verse in the context of the one before. Here we have shepherds in the biblical region of Bethlehem, watchmen of the night who experience the angel, the messenger of God.

Here is the take-home message. Why did the inspiration of the Lord come? Because the shepherds were keeping watch over their flock by night. They were doing exactly what they should have been doing in their place and time. They were doing their job! They were not seeking out a sign. They were not looking for a miracle. They were making life a constant quest to bring all things into one and present it to God. The angel came precisely because they were tending to their job, however mundane and insignificant it might seem to the world.

You might say the shepherds brought forth the angels. Causality becomes murky.

In addition to the messenger, they suddenly see the glory of God ("a multitude of the heavenly host") surrounding them. This can happen to each one of us in certain moments. This rarely occurs in the broad strokes of history, but most often in the quiet gestures which show the wonder of God's working through His creations and His creatures. The glory is the brilliance, the clarity, which surrounds us in our life if we are but shepherds, if we tend to our flocks, if we seek to have our life in order.

"And they were sore afraid." This is more or less how it is usually translated. The Greek is *phobon megon*, a mega-phobia, a humongous avoidance. Here the Hebrew helps us. The word translated as "afraid" or "terrified" is the Hebrew *yir'ah*, having a root identical with the word "to see." A proper translation must render this sense of seeing something that is astonishing. I suggest words like awesomely eye-opening, blinded-by-light, overwhelmed-by-insight. *Yir'ah* conveys an awe-inspiring wonder that breaks the receiving vessel, a joy that cannot be contained–like an electrical charge that shatters the capacitor. It conveys a glimpse, if only for a moment, into eternity — a glimpse from my hidden depths into the hidden depths of heaven, into the hidden depths of another world. When doing what we should be doing, we see God's hand and are overwhelmed.

One last thought from the end of the narrative: "And the shepherds returned." They went back from whence they had been. But they were not the same. Now what they do is to give glory and praise to God. For they had first heard (and acted upon what they heard), and subsequently they saw (after they had begun to walk in faith). Experience confirms the message from God. When we take in the message and follow the Word, then confirmation follows.

It is for you to choose which way you take in life. Decide if you want to be a modern economic man, calculating the advantage of all things, or if you want to acknowledge your heritage as a child of God. If the latter, then your interest in your flock is in its value as a sacrifice, as a gift to be taken back to God, and your goal is to raise up a "perfect sacrifice."

Do your job in the field in which you are put, hold steady through the night and God's word will come — with its accompanying glory. Listen up, then go look for yourself, and the experiences will come to you such that you can glorify God and praise Him for that life experience.

31 A babe in swaddling clothes
Christmas Program – 12/22/96

In this season we contemplate the birth of the Christ child, and reflect what it means that He has come into the world, into our life. In Luke, chapter 2, verse 12, we read: "And this shall be a sign unto you; Ye shall find the babe wrapped in swaddling clothes... ."

A sign is an indicator, a guidepost along the way, in this case, the way through our earthly sojourn back to our Heavenly Father. A sign is a token, a marker, a help from the eternal for us in our mortal condition.

A babe is the beginning of mortal life. The babe is open to everything, receptive to all things, dependent upon others for care-giving and protection, for nurturing and guidance. The babe is the youngest of those of whom the Savior says, "of such are the Kingdom of Heaven."

Swaddling clothes are what is wrapped around the babe. It is the material of this world which provides the envelope for the babe. "Swaddling clothes" is the totality of this world which envelopes our eternal soul from the moment of its emergence in human form. "Swaddling clothes" includes all strivings initiated, all appearances taken on, all positions gained, all achievements made, all desires realized.

"The babe wrapped in swaddling clothes" is an eternal sign. It tells the shepherds of Judea where and how they will find the baby Jesus. It tells us how Christ is with us throughout our mortal days. He is purity wrapped in all human aspirations, all appearances, all achievements.

I emphasize all, and make explicit its scriptural basis because, I fear, we tend to gloss over this. We have agency; we make choices; we agonize over these choices. We ask if we have chosen well or chosen foolishly, if we have done right or done wrong. We agonize over our choices, and then live in agony over the apparent result of our choices. We second-guess our decisions, we reproach ourselves; we regret what we have chosen, what we have done with our lives. We regret what we have not done, and rue what we have done. We ask for explanation of happenings which appear inexplicable, and for consolation from grief which feels inconsolable. We live in vivid awareness of the evil to which we have succumbed, of the cowardice we have displayed, of the human frailty to which we have yielded. And we doubt ourselves and we doubt our worthiness. Too often we also loath ourselves and are disparaging of the divinity with which God has infused us.

It is to us in this condition of doubt and agony that the angel of the Lord brings this message of a sign. To you, in your self-reproach and self-loathing, comes the Good News: the purity of God's gift comes wrapped in all that the world is, in all!

You know that you have enveloped yourself in the trappings of the world. You have acquired pride and prejudices. You have taken wrong turns, made foolish slips, not taken opportunities to do good deeds and to speak kind words when they presented themselves. You have partaken of the fruit of the Tree of Knowledge of Good and Evil. You have eaten good, and you have swallowed evil.

What are the eternal consequences of your choices? I borrow the words Isak Dinesen puts in the mouth of General Loewenhielm at the conclusion of Babette's transcendent feast.

"We tremble before making our choice in life, and after having made it again tremble in fear of having chosen wrong. But the moment comes when our eyes are opened, and we see and realize that grace is infinite. Grace, my friends, demands nothing from us but that we shall await it with confidence and acknowledge it in gratitude. ... See! that which we have chosen is given us, and that which we have refused is, also, and at the same time, granted us."

You agonize over your choices, but God knows why you chose as you did. You blame yourself for foolish decisions, but the eternal consequences are not yet recorded. You despair of missed opportunities, but might these have been a "wake-up call" for a coming opportunity that really matters? You flagellate yourself for returning to the trough of sin, but God knows how that, too, will be turned to good in His eternal plan.

What should you change of what your life has been? How should you use that one imagined magical wish? Do you wish for freedom from poverty? For no more hatred in the world? For understanding of this or that? The answer to this has been given to me: wish that absolutely nothing be changed. To change anything in God's creation is to presume we know better than God what He is doing in the world. To demand more understanding than God gives us is to offend the sanctity of his mysterious goodness.

Do not take the word of grace as justification for future evil intent, nor as an excuse from the need for present repentance. But in regard to what has unfolded in times past, I tell you, in the spirit of the coming of Christ, that you can do no better than to praise God and give Him the glory for all that has been. God knows how to work all things for good — even what we call our imperfections, errors and sins. And as a sign of God's grace, we are given the babe wrapped in swaddling clothes.

As the general concludes: "Ay, that which we have rejected is poured upon us abundantly. For mercy and truth have met together, and righteousness and bliss have kissed one another!" He is but singing the chorus of the carol sung by a multitude of the heavenly host. They, who know the world from the side of God, praise God and say, "Glory to God in the highest, and on earth peace, good will toward men."

In this season of our life, let us join the multitude of heavenly hosts. Let us praise God, sing out Glory to God for all aspects of our lives, for the totality of how we live. In this season, let God still your doubts, your fears, your self-reproach. Allow the Christ child into your life. Know that all things are hallowed for God, and that He works all things for good in the lives of those who love him. Peace be with you. Good will toward you. This I say in the name of our Savior, who comes to us as a babe wrapped in swaddling clothes. Amen.

32 Jesus of Nazareth
Sacrament Meeting – 12/19/99

Jesus of Nazareth. This phrase, like all in scriptures, conveys its message in the meaning of its words: the one who brings salvation from the fixed place of suffering oppression. Jesus, Joshua, "he saves." Nazareth, *Natsaret*, with a root meaning fixed in form, stuck in oppression, pain, and suffering.

Salvation does not enter our world at the holy temple in Jerusalem, and certainly not in a regional commercial center, be it in Nazareth — or an inlet of Puget Sound. Salvation comes to us in our place of pain and suffering. I do not have to tell you about suffering. You know. You know about physical infirmity, mental illness, deficits in character, laziness, and rebelliousness. You know about marital strife, separation from loved ones, worry about children, and about grand-children. You know about financial bondage, job insecurity, examination panic, social disgrace and low-self-esteem.

Though all trials are unique, we all have some kind of oppression and pain. No one is spared. We all live in a place of suffering. It is into this suffering that the means of salvation comes.

First comes a sign of hope in the heavens, a star in the East. Let us look up from our burdens below and see the promise shining in the heavens. The stars are most clear when the night is most black. Look up to the heavens in hope. Look up in hope.

Then comes a vision to the shepherds keeping their flocks in the field. Let us husband that which is entrusted to our care in our assigned field of labor. A glorious message comes to those honestly doing their daily work. Labor away at what you are given to do with love. Labor in love.

Wise men from the East bear gifts. Let us draw from our origin and bring the best of our legacy into the future. Buried in the rubble of the troubles and miseries of our shattered idealism are yet gems. Accept what you have been given in life with thanks. Accept life with thanks.

Finally, heavenly hosts join the choir. Let us give voice to that divine spirit deep within our soul. In our most evil hour, we are still children of God. Sing out in the holiness God gives you in joy. Sing out in joy.

The joy of salvation does not lie in the fact that we are free from adversity and suffering. The joy of salvation comes precisely through our being stuck in the trough of suffering and despair. It is precisely in this place that the message of salvation comes. Jesus comes to us in our hour of pain and doubt.

Salvation comes through enduring hope, eternal love, deep thankfulness, and divine joy.

My sisters and brothers, God above knows of our suffering — each of us in our own place and manner. God comes to us below and lives with us in the flesh. He takes on our pain, our panic, our doubts, our hate, our indolence, our weaknesses, our sins. He joins us, and He draws us to his bosom.

Rejoice in the joy of His salvation for us. Bring your hidden past to Him. Live out your life in His love. Look beyond your narrow world to have hope in what He brings, even now in your place of suffering.

This is the word of the Lord. This is the message of Christ coming into the world. This is your Christmas present. This is my wish for you in this and every season.

I say this in the name of Jesus Christ, the one who saves, the promised Messiah, who comes to us now. Amen.

Easter

Mormons give Easter a special significance as being not only the resurrection of Christ but also the season in which the Church of Jesus Christ of Latter-day Saints was organized.

33 The day before Easter
Ward Easter Sunday program – 4/16/95

Today we assemble as a ward family to observe the day of Christ's resurrection. We welcome the glorious light of Easter into the world, into our lives. We reflect upon what this Easter Sunday suggests about God's working in our lives.

This Sunday is the day in which the resurrected Christ appears. Death is overcome and our fear may likewise be vanquished. Mortality is surpassed. The tyranny of human law is conquered. Frailties of the flesh may be a thing of the past.

I would like to reflect on the day before Easter Sunday, on the Saturday of our life. Saturday and Sunday are recurring events in our life. Every week it is Sunday, Monday, Tuesday, ... Friday, Saturday. Saturday is the 7th day. It has been so ever since Creation. This is the day in which God pronounced His creation completed and in which He rested. He did not just rest, but (we read in Genesis 2:2): "God ended his work... and he rested... blessed the seventh day, and sanctified it."

On the Saturday before Easter Sunday Jesus lies in the tomb, at rest. There is no material hint but that this will be the sorry end of his life and work. On Saturday, the resurrection and all it brings is a promise by God and a hope in our heart. God knows what follows, so God is at rest. We are invited to share in this rest.

In partaking of the sacrament today we said "Amen" to the prayer that God might "bless and sanctify" the bread representing his body. We have His word that He has blessed and sanctified the day in which the bread emerged and was prepared. So we are merely saying "Amen" to what He has already done. We say "Amen" to the prayer that we may take on the name of Jesus Christ so that we "may always have His Spirit to be with us." What does this mean practically?

Although our knees may ache, our joints stiffen and our memory shortens, we may yet have His Spirit. Although we may be apprehensive about exams and worried sick about job prospects, God has secured what we need. He is at rest. Although we may be uncertain about the outcome of our pregnancy and the well-being of our children in an uncertain world, God has already counted the generations that follow; they are already known to Him.

God is at rest. We don't see the outcome, but God has completed His work. Our task is to love Him, to hope in His promise, to have faith in His word.

One other aspect of this Saturday from the Jewish tradition. For God it is a day of rest, for us it is a day of struggle. Saturday is the 7th day. The Hebrew for 7 is *zayen*. *Zayen* means sword. The 7th day is the day of the sword. It is a day of struggle, of contention, of conflict, of war. This refers not only to the wars between nations and persons, but to the ongoing war within us, our fight with our own good and evil.

Let me draw your attention to a detail about the creation account. Each period of creation ends with a formula: "And the evening and the morning were the 1st day." The formula is applied up through the 6th day. But when you look for it at the end of the 7th day, you do not find it. It is absent. This is because the 7th day has not ended. We live in the ongoing 7th day. We are expected to struggle.

What is our struggle? The particulars vary with the individual. For some of us, it is an ongoing war to find time for our secular study and to keep our spiritual life growing. For many of us it is the fight to balance our ambition for position and honor with our need to serve unobserved. For almost all of us it is the need to curb our urge to gossip. All of us need to fight to maintain our resolve to reform our life. It is so easy to rationalize our efforts when we fail to make the most of the opportunities God has given us.

So the fight goes on. We are engaged in this war with no hard evidence that it will ever be otherwise. All our experience notwithstanding, we are invited to join God in His Sabbath rest, to live in His assurance that the very next day will bring something we have not yet experienced but which is already prepared for us. God's creation is complete; He can rest. When we live in His Word, we can let our own minds rest. We need to fight our wars and persevere in our struggles. But we have God's sacred Word that He is ever mindful that we live under the sign of the sword. Jesus lies in the tomb but the unexpected awaits The Anointed. We may not recognize Jesus alive in us, but God knows what will come of our struggles and God is at rest. We are invited to join His rest.

34 The message of Easter
Easter Sunday at University Ward – 4/11/04

First, a word of reassurance on how long I am going to drone on. I know that this is Sunday meeting time, and I know that you know you should be focused on lofty spiritual matters. But I also know where your heart is. There is a timeless universal quality to youth.

It has been some 200 years since Goethe penned his *Faustus* with the scene of Dr Faust with Wagner outside the gates of the town. But the sentiment is timeless:

> "Looking backward towards the town see
> Forth from the cave-like, gloomy gate
> Crowds a motley and swarming array.
> Everyone suns himself gladly today.
> The Risen Lord they celebrate,
> For they themselves have now arisen
> From lowly houses' mustiness,
> From handicraft's and factory's prison,
> From the roof and gables that oppress,
> From the bystreets' crushing narrowness,
> From the churches' venerable night,
> They are all brought out into light ....
> Here is the people's paradise,
> Contented, great and small shout joyfully:
> 'Here I am Man, here dare I to be!'"

[or, so much better in the German]
"Hier bin ich Mensch, hier darf ich's sein!"

Goethe knew: we first realize our humanity when we emerge from the confined space in which we wrap ourselves and venture forth into the wide world. And we first realize our divine potential when we venture from our egocentric concerns and let God unfold the core of who we are.

I would really like to take my text from Gordon Lightfoot. I'd sing it, but you really don't want to hear my singing voice.

> "The soul is a rock, and the rock will not be moved
> When nothing is disputed, then nothing is disproved
> For the seeds of the earth that were planted long ago
> still yield a better harvest than the rock was prone
> to grow."

We have a divinely assured potential, which we shrink from realizing. We hesitate to become the person that we could. We are apprehensive of allowing our inner divinity to unfold.

And why? All of us have our own reasons, that is, our own excuses.

– It is presumptuous to flaunt our talents.
– We would be too embarrassed if we failed in public.
– My mother did not raise me that way.

The message of Easter that I would highlight is: He is risen. And thereby He is our model and our facilitator. And there are other worthy themes:

– Christ's agony in Gethsemane is worthy of all the reflections given to it.
– His suffering is as agonizing as portrayed. Recall Jesus's lament: "If Thou wilt, remove this cup!"
– The empty tomb is a worthy symbol; it is the earthy imprint of the eternal glorious fact: He is risen.

But the message I would underline today is: He is risen. We partake in Christ's glory when we too rise up. And in rising up we come closer to the realization of our divine potential.

So my exhortation on this Easter morn is: Rise up!

Rise up from your petty concerns. Let your worries about how you might appear to the world fade into your effort to do the work you have to do. Live in the divine light of your eternal potential rather than in the reflection of your friends and family, who might judge you by what they have seen of your actions rather than what they might hope of your potential.

Rise up from your lack of faith. Trust that God would not allow your current life assignment if He did not simultaneously give you the means to see it accomplished.

Rise up from your covetousness, from your seeing the talents and advantages of those around you while not trusting your own intuitive sense of solving your life problems your way.

Rise up from your sense of insecurity which paralyzes your willingness to step forth and act.

Rise up!

My testimony is that Christ is as alive in us as we will permit – and He is always more involved that we are prone to recognize, and sometimes more involved than we consciously desire.

My Easter wish is that each of us be more open to Christ, more open to letting Him into our lives, more aware of His quiet pleading with our soul, more mindful of His being in the lives of those around us.

This I pray, in His name, on this day when we observe His rising from the tomb. Amen.

35 The fulness of the resurrection
Easter Sunday – 3/30/97

This is Easter morn, the resurrection of Christ. Jesus is risen. The bands of death are broken. Faith triumphs over doubt. Joy overcomes despair. We bask in the light and truth of spring. The darkness of night recedes, the light of day ascends.

Today we celebrate the vindication of life, faith, confidence, and light. This is the positive side of death, doubt, despair, and darkness. Both belong to the totality of life. Reflect upon a Rembrandt portrait. It is precisely the blacks, grey, and browns that give power to the contrasting light.

Living in the totality of life means considering the utterances of Good Friday alongside the events of Easter Sunday. In the Garden of Gethsemane, Jesus says, "My soul is exceeding sorrowful, even unto death." And he prays, "O my Father, if it be possible, let this cup pass from me. [Matt 26:38-39]" On the cross he utters, "My God, my God, why hast thou forsaken me?" [Matt 27:46] Even the perfect man gave voice to sorrow and despair.

Christ was a sacrifice without sin, a lamb without blemish. He deserved none of the punishment and pain that befell Him. We sitting here cannot say as much. We are more like Limhi's people in the Book of Mormon, who were delivered from bondage by departing into the wilderness. [Mosiah 22].

Consider how they fell into bondage. Limhi's grandfather, Zeniff, was "over-zealous," which allowed him to be deceived by the cunning and craftiness of King Laman [Mosiah 7:21]. Being "over-zealous" resulted in their being taxed with "a tax which is grievous to be borne." The accountants and lawyers in the congregation may note this was a flat tax — a flat 50%, with no exemption for home mortgage payments. The people of Limhi also saw their brethren slain and their blood spilt in vain–directly tied to their collective and individual iniquity and transgressions. [Mosiah 7:24-25]

A flight from bondage by departing into the wilderness elicits the image of Israel in Egypt. Consider how Israel came into bondage. Judah persuaded his brothers to sell Joseph into Egypt. The biblical account lets us read between the lines for the motivation — except for envy, which is made explicit. So each of us has our own reading. I suspect most of us will insert jealousy, some greed, a few sanctimonious self-righteous posturing, and a few, clinging, co-dependent favoritism. Not a pretty picture of who we are.

These petty human motivations (envy, greed, self-righteousness) are also included in the totality of the resurrection. These, too, rise from the grave and find their place with God. When you recognize such motivations in you, you do need to yield them to the redeeming grace of the Lord: admit them, rue them, repent of them, do them no more. But you do not need to be grieved nor angry with yourself — because God knows our way and leads us in His path. This is not just Bishop Clark's reading. This is scripture. Joseph, on revealing his true self to his brothers, says: "Now therefore be not grieved, nor angry with yourselves... for God did send me before you to preserve life... So now it was not you that sent me hither, but God." [Genesis 45:5-8]

On this Easter morn, let us recognize God in our life. Let us live in the assurance that He sends us on our way, even in our sins and weaknesses. We need not be grieved nor angry with ourselves. We do need to recognize the hand of God in the preservation of our life, the totality of our life, our eternal life.

Mother's Day

Mother's Day has a special place in the Mormon church. At best, it is a touching tribute to the service and sacrifice of mothers. But it can be a painful experience for unmarried and infertile women.

36 — The mother's sacrifice
Mother's Day – 5/12/96

We gather today on the most trying day in the Mormon liturgical calendar. Many good saints deal with this day by simply staying away from church. For the last two years I found a legitimate excuse to be not only out of the state but on the east side of the Mississippi — and I would be there again this year but my two counselors threatened to quit if I did not show up and take my fair share. Why was I away? Basically I didn't want to be subjected to one more pro forma sermon on how mothers are wonderful, how their mothers were more wonderful, and how the pioneer mothers were most wonderful of all, and (by implication) how we should all feel belittled that we don't measure up to mighty standards of bygone days, and how we should feel deep shame about our negative thoughts and profound remorse about our downright rebellious feelings in regard to this whole motherhood thing.

I desire to convey comfort and hope to those who feel pain on this day, but many who carry the most pain are not here. So I need you who are here to carry my message. Not my words, for these are uniquely mine — elusive, convoluted, and obtuse, if not downright confusing. I want you to carry the message of comfort and hope in your walk, in your unspoken deeds, in your desire to do good — something I shall clarify in the last minute of this talk.

Today is Mother's Day. A mother is a female parent. So let us consider the concept female, and its complementary concept male. Here I want to talk of eternal verities. I do not want to be diverted into temporal concepts of equal rights, fair pay, power in corporate structures, etc. And I do not want you to make a quick and easy equation with a host of contemporary issues — which do deserve our thoughtful deliberation as citizens and informed voters. I am just not addressing them from this pulpit.

To refresh my theology about the eternal nature of male and female, I go down to the nursery. We have able Sunday School teachers in this ward, but the toddlers are closer to the source. In the nursery I find both the male and female side of my nature. I act in a male capacity when I stand by the door to bar exit and to keep the yung'uns from their misguided striving for liberty and freedom. I impose limits and enforce rules — with intent to guard and to protect. I am the warrior at the gate, keeping the child from temptations and dangers outside, and keeping external evils from its world.

I act in a female capacity when I hold a child in my lap to quiet its apprehensions, when I comfort and reassure, when I nourish and feed. For us, God is like a male when God insists upon perfection, remains an inscrutable, unfathomable mystery, imposes constraints, and does not even pretend to explain why. For us, God is like a female when God bears us in the womb, feeds our body and soul, holds us close, and lets us feel warm and cuddly.

God acts in perfect unity, but we cannot conceptualize perfect unity because we are imperfect. So we are given different names for different facets of our experience with God. The name of God who accompanies us through life is Jehovah, a Hebrew word with a feminine ending. This is in contrast to Elohim, which has a male ending. Jehovah designates a female. Now do not walk out saying I said God is a woman. I am not writing dogma for the church. I am telling you about my experience in the nursery of life.

To avoid getting hung-up on what I am trying to say, consider God not as a being (who is beyond our mortal comprehension) but as a body of functions. One set of functions is to preserve unity, to keep a complete wholeness, to maintain perfect harmony — for less than complete is less than perfect, and harmony is the resonance of perfection. A second set of functions is creation of the universe and of all subsequent creative acts. We share in creation, we act in the image of God whenever we create: human bodies through procreation, poems by Milton and plays by Shakespeare, doggerel by moon-struck teens, and scrawling by nursery toddlers. The male function is to hold all things in one, to be perfect — even as your Father in Heaven is perfect. The female function is to create, to bring all things to One.

I shall put it to the Primary children. Children, I shall tell you a story, a variant on the story of the war in heaven. One day God (in a female function) says, "I want to create a world." God (in a male function) says, "Don't do it, it would disturb our domestic bliss and tranquility." This is the conversation your parents had before you were born. Do not think that it was just your mother that wanted a child. Your father did too, but it was he who gave voice to the costs. "It will take something out of us, it will mean being awake at night and not being free to dance late at the Celestial Gold and Green Ball, or go to the All-sector Galaxy Playoff games without getting a sitter for the earthlings. It is knowing that the kids will be unappreciative of our gifts, demanding of their rights, and finally conclude that they are more clever than their creator and ought to run their own lives. They won't take our advice. They won't even call up except when in need of more money. They'll read scriptures for self-justification instead of guidance, and use prayer to beg rather than as a dialogue. Don't do it!"says the male function.

But the female (in all of us) says, "I must create because that is my nature." The male replies, "Creation expects too much. The children will flee, despairing in being abandoned, then reckless in their sense of self-sufficiency and finally destructive in their willful self-determination. They will raise a tower of confusion, ripen in iniquity and be cut off from the face of the earth. They'll ruin the environment, fight among themselves, bring on their own Götterdämmerung. It's too much to ask." It is then that the female says, "Alright, then I myself will accompany creation and go through all that my children go through. I shall be with them in all their doubts, all their stupidities, all their pain, all their suffering. Everything!!!" Then the male says: "This will satisfy the intrinsic need of perfection and harmony. Go forth!"

My experience in this nursery of life is that the God who accompanies me every day of my life is a gracious provider, full of tender mercies and loving acts of attention and care. This is nothing less than what any good mother would ever hope to do. Please do not get hung up on gender-specific words, and do not get lost in philosophical nitpicking. Feel the loving, maternal arms of God around you, and know the paternal righteousness of God protecting you.

We are in the image of God in our willingness to take on the sacrifice intrinsic to the act of creation. We create bodies for babies. We create church talks, work projects, theses for papers, quilt designs and floral displays. We devise winning plays and strategies for beating Seattle traffic. All this is creation. All this involves time, thought, and devotion — in a word, sacrifice. All this we celebrate this day.

One final plea. Creation is innovation, it is "doing it your way." In order to celebrate creation we must be willing "to boldly go where no man has gone before." This means to be willing to have your four children before you are 24 — despite all sorts of folks disapproving for all kinds of reasons. This means to be willing to forgo having children until you are over 34, or not have children at all — despite all sorts of folks disapproving for all kinds of reasons. This willingness to do it your way is your creative act and involves a commensurate sacrifice.

My plea is for us to leave judgment to God, to our Father in Heaven who preserves perfection and harmony. My plea is for us to support and comfort one another — even when we do not comprehend why another acts as she does. It is painfully hard to decide to leave your child in order to take up a job outside the home. And it is hard to forgo the second paycheck and miss the comradeship, adventure, and social rewards of working outside the home. It is painfully hard to forgo marriage rather than accept less than someone who seems your eternal worth. It is likewise painfully hard to decide to leave a man who has consistently not kept his marriage vows and demonstrates no intent of doing so. And it ain't always so easy to stay married. Ask my wife!

Each of us suffers and sacrifices — each in our own way. Let us walk alongside one another in solace and comfort. Let us live as Jesus lives. Let us love with a love worthy of our God in whose image we are made and in whose image we are invited to act. I pray this to Elohim in the name of Jesus, who has become our Redeemer.

Funeral Addresses

Funerals of Mormons are usually held in the chapel of the local congregation unless another place is more appropriate. The bishop of the deceased member conducts these services but usually does not speak extensively unless specifically requested by the family of the deceased.

37 God's grace in a time of loss
Funeral of Ethan Baker – 7/20/94

My remarks today are intended as a gift to all who loved Ethan and mourn his passing, particularly to Jill and Evan. I offer a statement of faith, and share an observation.

I have faith in a God who looks out for us and provides all that we need. I hold that our Father in Heaven provides all and wastes nothing.

This is a statement of faith, somewhat like my faith when I open up the box containing a put-it-together-yourself bookcase and see all those boards and the little plastic sacks of screws and fasteners. Only God gives us more than a bookcase. He is building His temple, His house, which is the tabernacle for our soul. He brings everything needed to build this temple, all the building blocks, no extras and no deficits, all the necessary time, no more and no less, all the necessary experiences, no more and no fewer. This is my faith.

I have observed that what we have come to call "Nature" seems wasteful and what we call "Fate" seems capricious. Crab grass overruns my flower beds and my orchards never bloom. Cawing crows proliferate and bald eagles are endangered. Some old people, despairing of life, linger on in wasted bodies, and the vibrant life of a beloved four-year-old comes to an end. I do not see a box of neatly-sealed plastic sacks filled with exactly what I think each particular person needs in order to put together his or her unique life.

When a field of golden wheat ripens and its grains dry to compact kernels, we anticipate the harvest and the bread that will feed us through the long winter. When the sturdy oak decays after giving protective shade for centuries, we say it has fulfilled its purpose and hew it down for the fire that will give warmth in the dark of the night. When my father dies in his nineties, the children gather, rejoice in the fullness of his life, and count his great-grand-children. But when the mortal life of a four-year old is cut off, it seems wasteful and capricious.

My observations in this life do not seem to confirm my faith. I have to hold my faith in spite of what I see here. I see cut short the life of a child, full of potential, loved by his parents. Their fervent hopes and prayers seem futile. Likewise futile seem the dedicated and devoted care of nurses and physicians trained in the best of modern medicine.

This disparity of faith and observation breeds doubt, pain and suffering. And we should never fall into the temptation of underestimating the depth of this pain and suffering. When a parent's love is insufficient to preserve and protect her young, the pain pervades God's creation. I have seen this pain in the scurrying about of ants when their disturbed anthill leaves their eggs exposed. I have heard this pain in the plaintive moaning of a mother cow when her newborn calf does not arise from its amniotic sac. And I have felt this pain most exquisitely in the noblest of God's creations, His children, those created in his image and likeness.

The pain of loss is directly proportional to the depth of attachment. The Power who arranges our times and seasons set me alongside Evan and Jill when Ethan's leukemia was diagnosed last November, and again at Ethan's passing last Saturday. I have been with them in their pain. We should not misunderstand Jill's saying, "You'll always be my boy." Nor should we misinterpret Evan's holding Ethan through the last hour and voicing, "I never believed we would lose him."

These are not expressions of denial. I know that both Jill and Evan have wrestled for months with the uncertainties of prognosis. No, these are expressions of a love that transcends time and space, a love that penetrates heaven itself. These expressions say, "As I love without limit so my pain seems limitless. Just as I put no bounds on the potential of life with Ethan, so I find no bounds to my grief at his loss."

Pain and grief of this magnitude approach the divine. Such pain and grief give us a glimpse of the pain and grief that our Heavenly Father feels for us when we separate ourselves from Him and when we limit the potential of our eternal life. The pain and suffering of this world is so great that it would be absolutely overwhelming, except for the grace, the loving-kindness that accompanies the creation. In our Christian faith we believe that the sins of the world, the apparent waste and capriciousness, are borne by the Son of God. The Messiah is born of Mary, who, according to the old hallowed tradition, is born of Anna, the Greek form of the word meaning "grace." This grace is the divine love that accompanies the creation; her child is the pain that brings forth the Messiah who shows us how to take God's creation back to its Maker. We participate in the salvation of the world when we bear the pain of our life in faith and grace.

The pain of a loss such as Ethan's passing defies description or comprehension. So let each of us feel free to express that loss in our own way for as long as we need. Some of us cling to the sweet, and bitter-sweet, memories of Ethan and hang on to the mementos of his life. Some put our agile minds to work to try to figure out the whys and what-ifs. Some protest the loss and cry the injustice to the high heavens. Some busy ourselves with the practical work of this world, seemingly oblivious to this death.

Some retreat into inscrutable silence, silence that might mistakenly be taken as criticism by any person prone to unnecessarily take on guilt. Many of us dip into several of these modes of expression, often uncertain exactly what we do feel and what we should do.

It is not for us to judge the manner of another's mourning. In these latter days the Lord God has told us to bear His tidings until the day comes when He will come Himself "to recompense unto every man according to his work, and measure to every man according to the measure which he has measured to his fellow man." We are judged as we judge others. We are called "to mourn with those that mourn; yea, and comfort those that stand in need of comfort, and to stand as witnesses of God at all times and in all things" What do we do when our faith finds no ready confirmation in our observation of life? Either we yield to what we see and die in our despair, or we stand as witnesses of God.

I have confidence in a day of restoration — when our vision will be clear, when sense can be made of the inscrutable, when we may count our pain as joy and our suffering as opportunity.

But that day is not yet now. Now we live in a vale of aloneness, see through a glass darkly, and walk in faith.

Sisters and brothers, let us join hands, let us embrace, let us comfort one another. Let our lives show that love which God has given His creation, and let us live in the faith that God has put in us.

Ethan, you may rest assured, is now in good hands. In my simplistic way I imagine Ethan at this very moment cuddling in God's arms, feeling at home there precisely because of a memory of such cuddling here. May each of us feel held in these same arms until our own day comes.

I pray this in the name of the Messiah, the Love of God Manifest, the Grace That Sustains Us, until we return to our Creator who gives life and takes life — all in his supreme wisdom for his divine purposes. Amen.

38 The binding of generations
Funeral of Lucile Adams – 10/15/94

It is a fitting tribute to Sister Lucile that the speakers today come from her family. This is what she would want. For as long as I have known her, her overriding concern was her family.

Personally, I knew her only as an elderly woman with a body that was bent and stooped but a mind that was clear and alert. She would raise her bent body and give clear voice in testimony of her ancestors and the heritage they left her. She kept before us the dedication of the generation that went before and their fortitude in overcoming their privations.

Sister Lucile was the model of a great-grandmother, and held that position in the ward. For almost all of us, she was the generation that went before. For those who knew her as a younger woman, not as a great-grandmother, and not even as a grandmother, but as a mother, I hear that she would speak of the basic things we now tend to take for granted in life: her satisfaction that her six children never went hungry and were always clothed.

Sister Lucile had a steadfast faith that the Lord would provide for those who trust in Him. She attributed this faith to her ancestors, and she wanted it passed on to her descendants. She was the link that binds generations. For the present moment she leaves us to join those she venerated, and I have faith that she will await patiently our joining her.

We take this occasion to share our memories about her and her legacy. We dwell upon the personal details of her life and upon the goodness of her heart. This is fitting, because on this occasion we, with her, approach our Creator and our God. I have faith that He has a personal interest in the details of our lives and judges each of us individually by a standard of goodness that we can only aspire to. He judges us by the intent of our heart.

We do tribute to Sister Lucile in approaching our God in the spirit that God reaches out to us. We perpetuate her faith when we leave this assembly with an increase in our personal caring for one another. We join her in binding generations when we listen to our heart and forgo judgment of one another by any external standard. In this caring and loving-kindness we approach God, even when we cannot fathom the immensity and grandeur of His creation.

May we do so I pray, in the name of His Son, Jesus Christ. Amen.

39 The fulness of life
Funeral of Hazel Zigler – 11/29/94

We gather to commemorate the passing of Hazel Zigler and to reflect upon her life and her legacy. And to reflect upon our own lives. I think of her as a model of the fulness of life. She lived a long life and she lived a full life.

Work, family, friend, these characterized her life. These were special in her life. And she handled all of them the old-fashioned way: she worked at them and she earned everything that came her way.

She took on the menial tasks in the kitchen at Relief Society functions, not claiming an elevated role because of her degree in dietetics. She cared for her own mother and she raised the young ones in her care as if they were her own–even down to making their clothing.

She was always involved in her church, sometimes filling two or three church callings at the same time.

She did not receive the honors and accolades of the world, but she was honored and loved by all who knew her, mirroring the extent she extended honor and love. She was the embodiment of the principles of hard work, self-reliance, honesty, diligence, inquisitiveness, and caring about people. Your presence here today testifies to that.

We have seen her life — but only the least part of it. She had a life before we came in contact with her, so she is better known by her family and friends who now reside in distant parts. She is likewise better known by the family and friends who have preceded her in mortality. In a similar manner, the greater part of our lives are hidden — even from ourselves.

We catch glimpses of her inner life in her soft voice, in the twinkle in her eye, in the orderliness of her house, in the beauty of her garden, the fragrance of her flowers, and in the constantly smooth running of her '74 dark brown Chevy.

Such a life is not lost. It might be temporarily hidden from view. But it persists.

She is eternally young. She just wore out her body so she had to move on to where she need not be slowed down by aging bones.

She lives in our memory. She lives in God's eyes. She lives in His loving arms.

We, too, have a life in our memory, and it is enriched by knowing her.

We, too, live in God's eyes, and we see something of our own potential in reflecting upon what He has provided for in her life.

We, too, live in God's arms. May we feel those arms a little closer when we reflect upon the love we feel for Hazel. May we carry this enhanced awareness of life away with us, even in this hour of mourning.

The grief we feel and share today belongs to the fulness of life, as does the warmth and love that comes to us from God through Jesus Christ.

I say this in His name, Amen.

40 Preaching to the choir
Funeral of Marie Wellman – 10/29/99

My talking to you is preaching to the choir. You know the meaning of the expression. The sermon is given to the believers.

The choir sits behind the pulpit. When you sit in the choir you have a different perspective. You see life, if you will, from the other side. You don't face the preacher, flailing forth, but you see the congregation and its response; you see them enraptured, inspired, ashamed, guilt-ridden, asleep... whatever.

You are also close to the organ pipes. That is fitting; music is holy and holiness is music. You sing praises to our Lord. Yours is the expression of a glad heart, and it is yours to gladden the hearts of all who come to the house of the Lord to seek His blessings and His inspiration.

Would that everyone belonged to the choir. Would that the entire congregation were here. Would that the entire community suspended its work-a-day activity and joined us. Anyone not here today is missing something, something of eternal worth.

We live in an age of ever-increasing acceleration. We have time-saving devices, greater productivity, almost instant communication — and less time, less peace and less quiet. What is wrong with this picture? And how do we right it? We begin by taking an hour, suspending the bustle and urgency of "earning a living" or "cleaning" or "shopping," and commemorate the passing of one of our dearly beloved. We allow ourselves to experience that life comes to us without our "earning" it, that we may live in purity without repeated "cleansing," that the essentials of life come to us as daily gifts from above.

These are precisely the lessons shown us by the life of Marie. In remembrance of her we are given a perspective on life, an eternal perspective. We can see that life, purity, and joy come to us — not as some distant reward but as living principles in our daily life.

The fullness of Marie's life cannot be summarized in a few minutes. However, as one single characterization of Marie, I suggest: Marie was a winner. However not just a winner but a leader of winners. I offer this not only as the prevailing metaphor for her life, but also as a literally true fact. What we tend to take as metaphors are often literally true. Marie was a winner.

You now know, thanks to Vicki's spilling the beans, that she was an avid contest winner. She was in no way a gambler, and was much more than an occasional contestant. She entered thousands of contests and she won hundreds of prizes. This characterizes her life. She did not win by occasional flukes, nor in some single desperate gamble. She won with a gaming spirit, and with such regularity that it shows more than luck. Her life shows perceptive insight, skill, and boundless energy.

When one of her grandchildren writes her biography, I hope she will have access to a list jotted down by one of her daughters of all her winnings, pages and pages of winnings. You know, thanks to Vicki, that she belonged to a national organization of contestants who played to win. She not only belonged, she was an active member, and, moreover, she was their president for a term. Those who competed seriously, those with a serious competitive spirit, recognized in her qualities such that they elected her to represent and to lead them. Consider the implications of that.

Consider how this statement characterizes her entire life. She was recognized as one to represent, to lead. In the church, Marie was Relief Society president for nine years under four different bishops. There are precedents, unofficial rules if you will, about this. A bishop serves for four to six years and in that time has two to three Relief Society presidents. Marie turned the rules around: she served nine years through four bishops. Guess who had the experience and the continuity of knowledge, both of what needed to be done and how things were done.

If we did not live in an age of acceleration, we would take the fullness of the day, having come prepared for a six-hour assembly and spend three-quarters of that time reciting the many incidences when she brought food to the hungry, succor to the poor, inspiration to the weary, comfort to the sick, and dignity to the dying. We would hear of the multitudinous times she brought reason into deliberations, restraint to undue exuberance, encouragement to undervalued thoughts, and unceasing energy to worthy projects. We would hear testimony after testimony of her beliefs, her words, her acts. We would hear of the efficacy of her prayers, the comfort of her glances, the aptness of her words.

But we are the choir, and we don't need the sermon. We may sit back and reflect upon what we know. And we may use the time following the formal service to share one with another what spirit we felt when she walked among us. Please do so — and take time to share your own reflection with her remaining family. This family, above all, is her enduring legacy here.

One final thought. I trust that all Marie has done in a full and rich life of loving service is chronicled in heaven, because there is no adequate account of it here on earth. This is all the more remarkable in consideration of what her situation appeared to be: an aging woman, widowed for the last two decades of her life, walking through life heavily, and without a car. This, too, is a literal truth which serves as a metaphor of her life. She was everywhere she needed to be for everyone who needed her. She transcended the awkwardness of terrestrial transportation. She has now transcended the encumbrances of the restraints of time and space. She has broken the bounds of appearance. I trust she has very recently received notice that she has won the big jackpot of life: life eternal with Keith, surrounded by those she loves and those who love her. Let us, even here and now, live with her there in that inner space that eludes appearance.

Let us live in the joy of life. Let us remember that being a "winner" is more than just luck, that service is more than just doing one's duty, that life is more than appearances. Let the remembrance of her life be a joy to us; let the occasional thought of what she has wrought bring a song to our heart; let that song burst forth in a fullness of harmony and love among us. We are, after all, the choir. Let the choral of our lives, like the anthem of Marie's full life, be a hymn to our Maker, who sustains us in everlasting love, love manifest to us in the life of his son Jesus, and in the life of his daughter Marie in her own time and way.

In His name and her memory I share this with you, Amen.

At the End

A bishop serves at the pleasure of the presiding authorities in the church hierarchy and the sustaining vote of the congregation. In this regard Mormon church administration tends to be "top-down" with members sustaining those proposed by higher church authorities.

The length of service of the bishop is traditionally about five years, but this, too, is subject to the wishes of the church leadership, often determined by the availability of other men to be called to this church position. Upon being discharged as a bishop, a man may be chosen to serve in a "higher" position in the church hierarchy, but often is absorbed again into the life of the ward.

41 Upon being released
Sacrament Meeting – 2/24/02

I knew this day was coming when the stake presidency's systematic study of the Handbook for Church Leaders came to the section on the qualifications of bishops. The footnote to the general rule that church leaders may not have facial hair specifies that stake presidents may make an occasional exception outside of Utah, southern Idaho and northern Arizona as long as the beard is white and *does not* exceed 3 inches in length. The 3-inch rule caught up with me.

I wish and pray that you extend to the new bishopric the kindness and prayers that my counselors and I have felt from you. Any goodness and wisdom coming through us is truly a reflection of your inner desires. I pray Bishop Brown and his counselors may feel sustained as we have for the past 8-plus years.

At this time I reflect upon the Declaration approved by the Continental Congress, July 4, 1776: "When in the course of human events, it becomes necessary to dissolve the bands which have connected them... a decent respect to the opinions of mankind requires that they should declare the causes which impel them."

This respect impels me to mention to you the fact that what has been a hobby for a couple of decades is now a calling. Some callings, you may know, come though church authority; others come directly. Direct callings cannot easily be demonstrated to others, but do need to be accepted. My current calling is to get serious about translating into comprehensible English some writings from the ancient Jewish tradition, which entail revelations and insights going back three to four millennia.

So you know I am not kidding about this like I was about the handbook rule on beards, I have brought a sampling from the six-linear feet of books sitting above my desk at home — and the German publisher continues to send me two or thee additional titles each year. Here's a sampling in my hand. ...And I did not bring in the 800+ page commentary on the Gospel of Mark, nor about forty other volumes. So, rest assured that I am not going to interfere with Bishop Brown's ministry. I am confident he will lead the ward in wisdom and grace.

Barbara says I may use half of her time. I would extend thanks to all who have given such love and support, starting with our stake president. You may, or may not, know that he extends bishops a level of trust and confidence that is rare in any organization. In more than a few meetings with stake leadership, I have heard him comment, "Well, I would not do that myself, but you pray about it and do as you are moved."

Your love has sustained me. I am mindful of private reservations about this and that, but I have been gratified constantly by your willingness to sustain in deed as well as in word. Bless you for that. Good things happen when we follow the Mormon way: everyone pitches in to build the community of saints — each in her season and in his way. Continue to love one another. Give it free expression when you see reasons to extend love, and practice forbearance, I pray, whenever you don't. God tends to the details of our lives more lovingly than we could ever imagine.

Finally, my testimony. For me listening to the melody of life is not just a metaphor; the melody carries the words of creation. I close invoking the name of Christ in the wish that each of us may live out the yearning of our heart. I shall play the tune, "Lord, I would follow Thee," I would invite you to hum the words.

42 Report: The nursery routine
prepared for the Annual Ward History – August, 2003

I'm writing this for all the kids. The little ones don't write so good as me. And the big people, who were supposed to do it, say they'll get to it – which means in a year or so. But when we kids decide to do something, we do it lickity split. So it's done before the big people notice and can get their hands on us.

Here's the skinny on the nursery. We've got a routine and we hold to it. And we got the big people pretty well trained. So we keep them moving along in the right order. Though we do have to remind them sometimes to keep on schedule: "Snack time yet?" "Can we sing now?" And if it's time to run around, and if the big people don't yet know it's time to run around, we just run around anyway.

We start with saying hello to our teachers and good-bye to our parent(s). No big deal for most of us. The young'uns mostly just go along with the program, 'cause they know whatever their parents do (mostly) is good even when they don't understand why. Some of us more clever ones raise a fuss at first. But it's mostly for show, and we stop it when we don't get a response. Though we do get held in a teacher's arms 'til it's clear our parents are really going to leave us for a while. Then we get involved with all the stuff around.

First we have what the big people call "Opening Exercises." It's no big deal, but it lets us know that we're in God's house and we're thinking of Him even while we're playing and singing. I take it the big people think it's good practice for all the meetings they say we'll be attending through all the years ahead.

The fun part is playtime. We got so many fun things. Sometimes there's new stuff, but mostly we like the same old stuff in the same old places. There's clay to squish, blocks to build up and then knock down, the bouncy-thing with the round balls, the play house, the play stove, the ramp with the little cars, and (not to forget) the table to hide under and then pop out and surprise the big people.

The best thing (not counting our parents coming back for us) is snack time. For this we quiet down. And we often get a book with pictures read to us. There's always juice or water (a little at a time in a paper cup), and always something good to eat. My mother brings in something every now and then, when she says it's her assigned time. And even if she forgets, it's no big deal because the nursery leaders have stashed away some crackers in a big plastic jar and some snacks in tear-open envelopes. The only rule is that we're supposed to eat up all that we ask for, which we always do — mostly!

After snacks we help clean up. But we don't let our parents know about this, because they just might begin to expect stuff like this at home. It fun to help out when it is new, but it's to be resisted when it's expected.

Lesson-time is short, and we learn a lot about loving families and Heavenly Father and Jesus who love us even more than our families do (though I can hardly imagine this!). During lesson time it's important to not let the teacher know that we're paying too close attention. So some of us run around a bit, or pretend to hide in a corner. But we still listen carefully and take everything in.

The lesson almost always has an activity with it. We get a paper or something to remind us of the lesson. We can color the paper or stick stickies on it. Stickies are easier for the little kids 'cause the color crayons don't always go the way our brain tells them to. We get to take the paper home, but sometimes we're so excited to see our parent that we forget the paper. No big deal, but some of us like it when our parent makes a little fuss about it.

Sing-song time is fun. We like the songs we know. And 'specially the songs we get to move our bodies with. It takes time to get down the word thing, but we can always bounce along with the music.

Best time of all is when we look up and see our mother's face. Maybe that's a little like it'll be when we go back to heaven. It's good when my mommy (or daddy) is not the last one to come for me. 'Cause it's kind of hard to see all the other kids get picked up and it's just me left with the teachers. (Though they never leave until I'm in safe hands again.)

So that's what nursery is like in the Seventh Ward.

43 Afterthought: On church governance
Sacrament Meeting – April, 2004

First, I want to use the pulpit to say "hello" to my special friends in the nursery. [a wave & "hi" to kids]
The differences between this and my past talks from this pulpit are: first, today my notes are not written out. There is no need if I am speaking only in a personal way and not in an official capacity; if I stray too far, Bishop Brown has the responsibility to stand up afterwards and correct my heresies. Second, Barbara has not pre-read and censured my remarks — so she is blameless.

My topic today is the genius of the church organization and the spirit of church governance. I shall consider two or three specific aspects rather than try to give a comprehensive overview.

One, consider how the president of the Church is chosen. The person is effectively selected at the time he is called to serve on the Quorum of the Twelve. The strict hierarchy rule means that all you have to do to become president of the Church is to somehow be called to the Quorum, and then merely keep your blood pressure down and keep breathing! If the Lord does not want you to become president, He sees that you do not keep breathing. No political intrigues or last-minute scheming.

Two, reflect that officiating in the name of the priesthood (outside of temple service) is limited to men. I will not get into many aspects of this arrangement, but I will point out that it means men are forced to assume some token responsibility. Lacking this, men, being who they are, would sit back on Sunday and mindlessly watch yet another football game and let the women run the Church like they run most everything else in life. (That extra half-chromosome really does seem to make a difference!)

Three, note the pattern of church callings to service in the ward. Anyone can be called to do most anything, and most everybody does something. And no calling is forever. If you are greatly unhappy with your bishop or Relief Society president, just keep living and coming to church; in a couple of years or so you will have a new leader. Now I've had teachers and leaders who were not my cup of tea. But I don't know all that goes into a given calling. Perhaps the person needed that calling at that time in his life, or maybe she spoke to the needs of someone else who was less able to delay having their spiritual needs met than I.

I have speculated that if I were a bishop in a BYU ward, I would make all callings by lot, drawing names out of a hat. I have noticed that the needs of the ward can be met through a number of different configurations. Some years a strong service and activity committee works wonders, and sometimes that function is taken up by committees within the quorums and Relief Society and Primary organizations. My fancy is that if the entire ward truly lived by the Spirit, then as bishop I could announce that everyone should pray for his or her assignment each week. Someone would come prepared to teach a given Primary class; someone would bring bread for the sacrament; someone would have hymns chosen. (Now you know why Barbara reads my talks, and why President Tucker did not leave as stake president before he saw me released.) Such an organizational scheme may seem far out, and I never would have seriously tried to do it, but I am only half kidding when I assert that we should be living such that it could be implemented.

My testimony is that God directs this church; this is both my conviction and my experience. He can work in different ways. I know the stories where the bishopric ponder a calling, get on their knees in prayer, and all arise with the same name on their lips. That is one way. But given that we held bishopric meeting before Sacrament Meeting, and often had ten minutes left before it was time to get to the stand, we would toss out some names to reflect upon in the coming week. Then we would all go home, and ask for our wives' reflections. Then we'd all come back with same name on our lips.

Seriously, I'll share a true anecdote. About every second or third year the bishopric would agree on a calling, and delegate Brother Lamb to issue it. The next week, Brother Lamb would start to apologize for not getting around to issuing the calling. I then faced a hard choice: should I allow him to continue to apologize, or tell him that since last Sunday I had learned that what we decided was clearly not the best choice. His negligence seemed to be inspired, even though he had no way of knowing it.

God has many ways to see His will effected. And we have many ways to reach Him. Sometimes it is on our knees; sometimes it is talking to Him while stuck in traffic ; sometimes even with a few cuss words thrown in. The supplications of an honest spirit reaches Heaven; I don't think the style is always so critical.

The answer to the question of how God responds to our petitions is the same answer to the question of how does the proverbial 400-pound gorilla act. The answer is: anyway he wants to act. Consider God's timetable for Jonah. God could have sent down thunderbolts or some persuasive argument. Instead, I speculate, God thinks out the timetable something like this: "So I ask Jonah to help me out. He'll not say no, but he'll run and take a ship in the opposite direction. So I allow enough lead time for him to walk to the coast, sail away, be taken in by the whale, repent, and get to

Ninevah precisely in time to proclaim My word when the time is ripe." Make no mistake about it; God's will shall prevail. The only variable is to what extent we will join in to promote Him having His will play out. I am impressed that we are often given the opportunity to stand in for God, to act in His name, to do His will. We bless babies, visit the sick, make home visits, look out for the welfare of His children. The formal organization is coordinated in the bishop's office, but most of the good work done in this ward does not appear on the agenda of the bishopric meetings.

I'll share one little example, that of welfare assistance. While I was bishop, for more years that not, more financial help was extended through private gifts than came from church funds approved by the bishop.

There is one mistake I'll own up to. That was passing on a copy of the Bishop's Handbook to my counselors. When I was first called, the counselors' copies of the book detailing church protocol and procedures had been lost. So for three years Brother Lamb was issuing callings to auxiliary heads. Then he read in the handbook that the bishop was personally to call the heads of organizations.

My eldest son, now an attorney, notes (quite correctly) that I had no need to have the handbook written out. I knew it from six decades of life in the Church. The basic recipe is simple: 20% historical precedent, 30% common sense, 40% forbearance, and 50% inspiration. I know this adds up to more than 100%, but hey, aren't we supposed to be giving more than 100%?

What applies in the Church also applies in our individual lives. God knows our life course, but He usually does not inform us in advance. So we have to live out our lives to know what will become of our lives. Be assured that whatever the situation we are in, God has foreseen this and has provided for its resolution. We do know what to do with our lives if we listen to the still, soft voice within. Or we can look at how events play out. The former course is easier on us, but God will get His message through one way or another.

I shall close and summarize with the first and last verse of the 23rd Psalm as rendered by the 17th-century cleric & Latin scholar, George Herbert.

"The God of love my shepherd is,
        and he that doth me feed:
while he is mine, and I am his,
        what can I want or need? ...
"Surely thy sweet and wondrous love
        shall measure all my days;
and as it never shall remove,
        so neither shall my praise."

Listing of sermons by date given

1 Appreciation and comments
  Upon being sustained - 8/08/93
2 Rights of the Priesthood
  Priesthood Correlation Meeting - 8/22/93
3 Pray by name
  Comment in Sacrament Meeting - 8/22/93
17 In the year that Uzziah died
  Sacrament Meeting - 8/29/93
4 On gossiping and backbiting
  Sacrament Meeting – 9/12 /93
28 Jesus comes
  Christmas Program - 12/12/93
5 Missing members
  Sacrament Meeting – 12/19/93
6 Notes on counseling by Bishops
  Seattle North Stake Presidency/Bishopric Meeting –
                                                    1/06/94
7 The Church
  Ward Conference – 4/17/94
37 God's grace in a time of loss
  Funeral of Ethan Baker – 7/20/94
12 Meaning of temple work
  Sacrament Meeting – 8/28/94
8 Reflections on leadership
  Leadership dinner – 10/2/94
19 The foundation of our life
  Sacrament Meeting – 10/9/94
38 The binding of generations
  Funeral of Lucile Adams – 10/15/94
39 The fullness of life
  Funeral of Hazel Zigler – 11/29/94

29 Mary's burden
    Christmas Day Sacrament Meeting – 12/25/94
9 Pattern your life ... the model of a community
    Ward Conference – 4/09/95
33 The day before Easter
    Ward Easter Sunday program – 4/16/95
18 Your personal relationship with God
    Sacrament Meeting, – 10/22 /95
30 Shepherds in the field
    Christmas program – 12/24/95
36 The mother's sacrifice
    Mother's Day – 5/12/96
13 Follow the prophet
    Sacrament Meeting – 11/03/96
14 Laws and commandments of the gospel
    Sacrament Meeting – 11/24/96
31 A babe in swaddling clothes
    Christmas Program – 12/22/96
15 The duties of members
    Ward Conference – 3/23/97
35 The fulness of the resurrection
    Easter Sunday – 3/30/97
20 Wrought upon and cleansed
    Ward Conference – 2/15/98
21 Understanding our relationship to scripture
    Sacrament Meeting – 3/22/98
22 On sacrifice
    Sacrament Meeting – 8/4/98
10 To bring our brethren again to thee
    Ward Conference – 1/10/99
23 The sound of *shin*
    Sacrament Meeting – 4/10/99
11 What we make of it
    Sacrament Meeting – 7/25/99

Listing by date

24 The short cut; do you really think there is one?
    Sacrament Meeting – 8/08/99
40 Preaching to the choir
    Funeral of Marie Wellman – 10/29/99
16 Two kinds of cookies; two sets of books
    Sacrament Meeting – 11/28/99
32 Jesus of Nazareth
    Sacrament Meeting – 12/19/99
25 A question without an answer
    Fast and Testimony Meeting – 1/02/00
26 Let us labor diligently
    Ward Conference – 1/21/01
27 Quiet and assurance forever
    Ward Conference – 1/21/02
41 Upon being released
    Sacrament Meeting – 2/24/02
42 Report; The nursery routine
    Prepared for the Annual Ward History
    – August, 2003
34 The Message of Easter
    Easter Sunday at University Ward – 4/11/04
43 Afterthought: On church governance
    Sacrament Meeting – April, 2004

Made in the USA
Columbia, SC
05 April 2023